D1809383

cooking with...

cooking

with**michael**elfwing

mc **Marshall Cavendish**
Cuisine

Photo credits: Michael Elfwing for all photographs except 'whats_on_your_plate' (jaylopex/SXC.hu), 'forkspoon' (inya/SXC.hu) and 'black_cow' (Thoursie/SXC.hu) Copyright © 2010 text and photographs, Michael Elfwing

Designer: Lock Hong Liang

Published by Marshall Cavendish Cuisine
An imprint of Marshall Cavendish International
1 New Industrial Road, Singapore 536196

All rights reserved

No part of this publication may be reproduced, stored in a retrieval system or transmitted, in any form or by any means, electronic, mechanical, photocopying, recording or otherwise, without the prior permission of the copyright owner. Permission requests should be addressed to the Publisher, Marshall Cavendish International (Asia) Private Limited, 1 New Industrial Road, Singapore 536196 Fax: (65) 6285 4871 E-mail: genref@sg.marshallcavendish.com Online bookstore: http://www.marshallcavendish.com

Limits of Liability/Disclaimer of Warranty: The Author and Publisher have used their best efforts in preparing this book. The Publisher makes no representations or warranties with respect to the contents of this book and is not responsible for the outcome of any recipe in this book. While the Publisher has reviewed each recipe carefully, the reader may not always achieve the results desired due to variations in ingredients, cooking temperatures and individual cooking abilities. The Publisher shall in no event be liable for any loss of profit or any other commercial damage, including but not limited to special, incidental, consequential, or other damages.

Other Marshall Cavendish Offices:
Marshall Cavendish Ltd. PO Box 65829, London EC1P INY, UK • Marshall Cavendish Corporation. 99 White Plains Road, Tarrytown NY 10591-9001, USA • Marshall Cavendish International (Thailand) Co Ltd. 253 Asoke, 12th Flr, Sukhumvit 21 Road, Klongtoey Nua, Wattana, Bangkok 10110, Thailand • Marshall Cavendish (Malaysia) Sdn Bhd, Times Subang, Lot 46, Subang Hi-Tech Industrial Park, Batu Tiga, 40000 Shah Alam, Selangor Darul Ehsan, Malaysia • Marshall Cavendish International (Asia) Private Limited. Times Centre, 1 New Industrial Road, Singapore 536196.

Marshall Cavendish is a trademark of Times Publishing Limited

National Library Board, Singapore Cataloguing-in-Publication Data

Elfwing, Michael.
Cooking with Michael Elfwing. – Singapore : Marshall Cavendish Cuisine, c2010.
p. cm.
ISBN : 978-981-4328-39-5

1. Cooking. 2. Cookbooks. I. Title.

TX714
641.5 — dc22   OCN665002090

Printed in Malaysia by Times Offset Printing

My late mother for her endless love and raising me to stand on my own feet.

My father for his commitment to giving me the best culinary preparation I could ever ask for.

Cheong Liew for being a mentor, friend and inspiration.

Mathias Dahlgren and Adam for showing me the best of Swedish produce, cooking, and respect for our Nordic heritage.

I thank Heston, Ashley, Kyle, Graham, Magnus, Otto, Ida and Kim for a memorable experience at The Fat Duck.

Mathieu Pacaud from L'Ambroisie for opening my eyes to French cuisine.

acknowledgements

contents

introduction

"

I have been fortunate in that I have had many wonderful food experiences throughout my life, growing up in a family where food and home-cooked meals were a central part of our lives, learning about European produce from my travels in Europe and working with chefs who inspired my passion for cooking. "

I grew up in Landskrona in the south of Sweden, a small coastal town known more for its frosty temperatures than its food or produce. My early interest in cooking was sparked by my mother's really tasty *husmanskost* (traditional Swedish fare). Memories of the food she cooked for my younger sister and me will always stay close to my heart and her influence can sometimes be seen in my recipes. In fact, whenever I am homesick, I make gravlax.

But it is my father who has been my greatest inspiration – he is a chef who has cooked all over the world, in restaurants, hotels, cruise ships and vineyards. I remember spending much of my childhood visiting him and waiting for him in the chefs' office, and being plied with sandwiches piled high with Nordic shrimp, or ham and cheese by the ladies in the cold kitchen.

When I was 16 years old, I went to Perth, Australia, to visit my father who had moved there. What was to be a six-month holiday turned into a seven-year stay and a love for all things Australian. I arrived in the month of October but it was only in April of the following year that I saw the first cloud in the sky. It was enough to get the northerner in me to want to live there.

My first job in Perth, which was also my first job ever, was with my father at a restaurant that he had taken over in a Swan Valley winery. It was called Little River Winery and Café, and it served rustic French cuisine such as terrines, duck confit and lamb pie. For the first three months, I did not do much more than mop the floor and wash the lettuce and the dishes, although I did peel a few vegetables and had a real chef's uniform and a set of knives. My father believes that to be a chef, you need to learn everything, and that as a chef you must love to clean – clean the kitchen, clean the food. Looking back, I can see that the time I spent with him in the kitchen gave me the best foundation I could ask for. Making sure that the label of every bottle, every can, every container faces out so that it is easy to read is a small thing that will allow you to do big things. And a well-organised kitchen makes it a lot easier to find what you are looking for. Working at a winery also gave me the opportunity to see how vintages are made. I didn't like wine when I started at Little River, but the winery's owners, Count Bruno de Tastes and his wife Jan, developed my interest in it by showing me how the grapes are picked, crushed, pressed, fermented and then aged. Together with my father, they also shared ideas on how to pair wine with food. To this day, I can picture in my mind the shiny vats of chardonnay and viognier; the cold cellar with barrels and barrels of shiraz and cabernet sauvignon. And although at first I could not tolerate the smell of wine and yeast, now I kind of miss it.

After five years at Little River, I moved to Adelaide and got a job in the pastry section at a restaurant called Bergerac. As Bergerac's owner was an organic vegetables purveyor, the produce we used in the kitchen was outstanding. I was part of a very passionate opening team there which included chef Julie

Ziukelis and chef Robert Paglia who taught me how to make a good cup of coffee. In our first year, we were rated the best new restaurant in the state.

It was at Bergerac that I met celebrity chef Cheong Liew. He invited me to work for him at his renowned Grange restaurant at the Adelaide Hilton, and as much as it was difficult for me to leave Bergerac, I could not say no to the opportunity. At Grange, I immersed myself in Cheong Liew's creative Oriental cuisine and learned about Asian ingredients, such as when to use light or dark soya sauce. Going into a kitchen and knowing nothing after coming from a restaurant where everything was familiar to me was a challenge. Fortunately, I was supported by executive chef Simon Bryant and a very committed team at the restaurant – most of us would start two or three hours before our shifts, just to get the food right. Sometimes, Grange sommelier Trevor Maskell would even take us to Barossa Valley winery Rockford to take part in their yearly harvest of cabernet sauvignon.

Then the opportunity to open Senses at Hilton Kuala Lumpur came up, and I packed my things again. Kuala Lumpur is a place I would probably never have visited if not for Cheong Liew, but when I arrived, I found myself quite at home. Living in KL is all about eating – Malaysians love to eat and they have the best food available to them at all times. I could also see that a lot of the ingredients used in KL were similar to those used in Adelaide, and that some dishes I had cooked there were actually Malaysian-inspired. At Senses, I had to show that I could deliver everything I had learnt before. Cooking for Malaysians is a daunting task, because this is their food and their heritage, just modernised and tweaked by Cheong Liew. The first menu was very Cheong Liew- and Grange-inspired; over the years though, the cuisine at Senses has evolved to take on more of my personality. The restaurant has hosted numerous guest chefs, from Australia's Luke Mangan and Greg Malouf, New Zealand's Jason Dell and Stephen Tindal to Spain's Paco Roncero and

France's Michelin-starred Christopher Coutanceau and Mathieu Pacaud. Some of them have become good friends and welcomed me into their kitchens; I have also been lucky enough to do a stage at The Fat Duck. My time at Heston Blumenthal's restaurant made me see that anything is possible – The Fat Duck's kitchen is very small but it is very organised, and everyone is 110 per cent committed to his or her job.

All these factors have contributed to my style of cuisine today, and through the recipes in this book, I hope to give you a taste of my journey and inspirations.

Smaklig måltid!

Michael Elfwing
November 2010

michael's *notes*

Entrée

When serving entrées you want to set the expectation for what's to come. At home, it is a great way to show off a little, too. You will get away with smaller portions and don't need to spend much on lavish ingredients. It also brings variety to your dinner parties. You can make a gorgeous salad using colourful lettuce and organic or heirloom vegetables. A lot of organic and heirloom vegetables come in colours and shapes we have forgotten. Purple carrots, multi-coloured radishes, tomatoes in all shapes and sizes, from the brightest green Zebra-striped tomato to the deepest purple, almost black Kumato. Serve these beautiful vegetables with a nice and smooth French dressing or arrange them with your homemade Wagyu bresaola for a perfect start to a lunch or dinner. Beetroot and scallop salad with warm goat's cheese is a colourful treat full of flavour and organic potential.

Soups

I love making soups, but to be honest I never used to like soup much. Soups as I knew them were either clear with a few vegetable cubes floating around, or thick and over-boiled with a swirl of cream for "good looks". It was not until I came to Asia that I got an eye-opener for soups. Take a bowl of laksa, for example, a labour of love. Twenty to 30 ingredients go into making the broth alone, then another six to ten ingredients are added in the bowl when you eat it. I have not even started on the flavour or texture yet, but those of you who know what I am talking about will all be nodding while reading this. My soups are influenced by these experiences, not necessarily in flavour but how I make and serve my soups. My seafood soup is based on French bouillabaisse, but I cook all the seafood separately and arrange them nicely in the soup bowl before I pour in the soup upon serving. This gives me the control to serve everything at its best. The seafood is freshly cooked and the soup is not over-boiled while the seafood is simmering in it. A seared and caramelised scallop tastes so much better than a boiled one right?

Texture is very important in my soups. You will find that almost all my soups have their fillings and garnishes cooked separately. This might seem intimidating, but allows you to make the soup a couple of days before you intend to serve it. This way you can plan in advance and simply cook the filling and heat the soup and serve.

Beef

I can talk about beef until the cows come home, I have been told. I have a great passion for beef and its potential. These days, when everyone is looking for ways to save money and spend less, it puts great pressure on chefs and producers. Most people want to eat a tender steak and pay as little as possible for it. The truth is that good beef is expensive; it takes a lot of time, space and money to keep cattle for beef production. I am very proud to know that there are farmers who still practise organic beef production and keep local breeds of cattle that are born and bred locally. I feel that Australian beef, Australian Wagyu beef and Meat & Livestock Australia are truly world leaders in their own field. They have set the standards so high that as consumers, chefs or gourmands, we can trust what we buy and eat when we choose Australian beef. Over the years, I have chosen to work very closely with Stanbroke beef. I love the flavour and texture of their beef, be it grain-fed or organic – it is really outstanding.

Genetics plays a large role in Wagyu beef; this is a different game altogether. Japanese beef and Wagyu beef are not to be confused. Both are very different when you place them next to each other. Their textures and tastes are also different. All these little details make up the big picture for chefs when we decide what to do with each type of beef and each cut of beef. I can eat and enjoy a grain-fed steak rare and just warm, but for Wagyu beef, I like to cook it so that the marbling starts to melt and release its flavour and aroma. I don't enjoy a rare Wagyu beef that has simply been seared and rested for the reason that it is not served at its full potential. Cook it gently and let that complex flavour of meat, fat, marbling, seasonings and cooking method mingle together and you will never look back again.

But the last note on beef, and what I feel most passionate about, is the so-called non-loin cuts. These cuts have the most flavour, give the best results when cooked right, and have endless potential. My recipes for Corned Beef, Braised Beef Cheeks, Steak and Lager Pie, and Spicy Oyster Blade Salad all use non-loin cuts and can be varied to the type of beef cuts that are available to you. For us chefs, it is very important that we influence and teach others how to use non-loin cuts. I give cooking classes regularly and the ones about beef sell out the fastest. I find that more and more people are starting to understand the importance of using the whole animal and to build a sustainable environment where we don't only use the simplest of cuts to cook.

From Land and Sea

These days, a lot of what we eat is farmed – be it poultry, lamb, venison or fish and seafood. I support farmers who go the extra mile to ensure that animal welfare is given high importance and that nature is not destroyed in the same process. I love to use lamb from Western Australia. Dorper Lamb is a product I can easily speak for. Its meat is the most tender and tasty I have come across. To be honest, most lamb racks and lamb loins are tender. But with Dorper lamb, the hind legs can be cut into steaks and the shank then braised for stews or pies. You get a wonderful round steak from an easy-carve leg of Dorper lamb that takes a maximum of 10 minutes to cook. No effort is required. The flavour of a lamb leg is something we can all relate to from our memories of roast lamb. But Dorper lamb has none of that strong lamb fat and lanolin smell when cooked.

I rub the whole leg with fragrant herbs and spices, roast it in the oven, then slice it up and serve. It doesn't get easier than that. Have a look at the recipes for Easy-carve Dorper Lamb leg and Melting Dorper Lamb shoulder. Maximum flavour and minimal effort.

Of course, in restaurants we use ingredients that people will question are sustainable or even farmed with the animals in mind. These days, customers demand what they want to eat, and not always what the restaurant wants to serve. This is a challenge that a chef has to learn to deal and work with. Foie gras and shark's fin are always topics of discussion on what's right and what's wrong, and we all have our own thoughts on this matter.

A lot of farmed fish and seafood we find today is close to wild and of equal quality, but with the benefits of not hurting the wild fish stocks in our seas and of giving nature a chance to recover. Look for fish that have been organically farmed or raised in their natural environment and you can't go wrong. Mussels, oysters, salmon, ocean trout, turbot, halibut, yellowtail kingfish and sure-to-come blue fin tuna are all great examples of how fish and seafood farming have evolved to meet customers' and nature's demands.

Snacks

Included in this book are my little secrets from the professional kitchen. They give a little insight into the modern cooking techniques we apply to create something unusual for our diners. The recipes include some unusual ingredients and terminology. I feel it is important to share and let people in to understand our work better. A lot of our guests are very curious and want to know our secrets, even if they are never to attempt the recipes themselves.

Desserts

Now, this is where things are getting sweet. I have a real sweet tooth. I can't decide if it is good or bad. I think it is mostly good. It gives me the inspiration to come up with desserts that I want to eat. My desserts are not loaded with sugar as you will see. I try to find combinations that work well together and make for interesting desserts. Try the Almond and Milk panna cotta which is low in sugar and fat. I like to use water in my desserts; it makes all the other flavours stand out rather than mask them. Dairy is very important in desserts. Buy the best quality you can find; the price will usually serve as a guide. You don't need bucketloads of it and the small portion you are going to eat in the end will make it worth the effort. Try the parfait recipes, foolproof ice cream made at home that can be made to suit your preference. Learn the technique and create your own flavour combinations.

Chocolates and Petits Fours

Chocolate is like dairy. You don't need a lot but make sure what you use is the best you can find. I use Valrhona chocolate in my kitchen. I find it is the best that is available from almost anywhere in the world. There is a large range – from white to dark and spicy, never sweet and always smooth and fragrant. Chocolate pralines are a joy to make. I think everyone should try at some stage. Buy some chocolate hollow forms from your local pastry shop or your favourite restaurant. I am sure they would be happy to sell you some. Then go home and flavour your chocolate with anything you like and start rolling pralines. These will make great little presents and your friends will be very impressed.

Petits Fours also have endless possibilities. Nothing is better than a few homemade treats to serve with a cup of coffee or tea when unexpected guests arrive. The ever-trendy Macaron is another Petit Four worth the time and effort. Make a large batch and freeze them. You will be the envy of your friends at any gathering if you bring your own homemade Macarons.

Cheese Notes

I have included some cheese notes of my favourite cheeses. No meal is complete without cheese, as the French say – and for me, it's a toss-up between cheese and dessert when I go out. Usually, I have both.

michael's notes

Michael *Elfwing*

is an innovative chef with an incredible amount of energy. He is constantly researching into what's best for his cooking.

A passionate student of the culinary art, he takes his art seriously and I am sure he will achieve his life's ambition.

Since the days when he worked in the Grange restaurant, I have always had great respect for him, and for his keen interest in wanting to learn from the Grange Kitchen. That is one of the reasons I invited him to join me in opening Senses restaurant in Hilton Kuala Lumpur. At the same time, I wanted him to have more exposure to multicultural Malaysian food. Since then, he has not only made Senses one of the best restaurants in Asia but he has also developed his own style of cuisine based on his constant search for innovative food. I wish him well in his endeavours.

CHEONG LIEW

foreword

Le souvenir d'une rencontre, d'un échange et surtout la découverte d'un parcours atypique, celui d'un jeune cuisinier européen, tombé amoureux d'un pays merveilleux. Officier dans un grand hôtel en Malaysie , trouver les produits, s'adapter aux goûts et coutumes locales et laisser parler sa creativité, est un challenge de tous les jours.

C'est pourtant avec talent que Michael arrive à concilier tous ces « ingrédients » pour offrir à ses clients une cuisine d'exception mélangeant influences européennes et asiatiques. Il est à l'image de sa cuisine : inventif, expressif et simple. Ce fût pour moi un grand plaisir de travailler avec lui et de partager nos connaissances et nos secrets.
Ce livre reflète sa personnalité, il est pour le lecteur une source d'inspiration et s'adresse autant aux profanes qu'aux professionnels. Avec cet ouvrage Michael distille son immense savoir-faire et enchante avec des recettes audacieuses, colorées, originales et accessibles.

Ce livre vous donnera le goût et l'amour de la cuisine.

MATHIEU PACAUD

A memorable *meeting,*

a chance to exchange creative ideas but most of all, the discovery of something quite exceptional.

That was my experience when meeting a young European chef, who'd fallen in love with a fabulous country.

As Chef de Cuisine of a fine dining restaurant, sourcing ingredients and adapting them to the local culture, without infringing on his culinary creativity, is a day-to-day challenge.

However, it is undoubtedly Michael's talent that allows him to bring together his "ingredients" and offer his customers an exceptional menu, influenced by both Europe and Asia. He is the image of his art; inventive, expressive and very approachable.

For myself, it was a pleasure to have worked with Michael and to have had the chance to exchange our culinary knowledge and secrets.

This book is a reflection of his personality and a source of inspiration, for both beginners and professionals.

Michael is sharing his knowledge and passion with a selection of bold, colourful, original and achievable recipes.

This book will give you the taste for, and love of cooking.

entrées

"When serving entrées you want to set the expectation for what's to come. At home, it is a great way to show off a little, too."

chicken liver pâté

1+1 hr   serves 10

600 g chicken liver
300 ml milk
50 ml cognac
150 ml port wine
6 shallots, finely chopped
1 tsp fresh thyme
600 g butter
6 whole eggs
sea salt and ground white pepper
red onion jam (*recipe follows*)

1 Clean the liver and remove the white sinew holding the livers together. Soak liver in milk and cognac for 1 hour. Remove the liver and pat dry on kitchen paper. Combine the port wine, shallots and thyme in a pot and reduce over medium heat until all port has evaporated and been soaked up by the shallots. Heat the butter over low heat and add the liver and shallots, cook gently until the liver is medium-cooked.

2 Pour the liver and butter mixture into a blender and blend until very smooth. Season with salt and pepper. Add the eggs one by one, once incorporated into the mixture, strain the mixture and pour into a terrine mould and bake at 140°C for 50 minutes.

3 Once cooked, let the pâté sit in the terrine mould overnight and unmould the following day or eat it straight from the mould with some crusty bread. Serve with red onion jam for extra bite.

red onion jam

1 hr   makes 1 kg jam

1 kg red onions
4 Tbsp olive oil
1 tsp crushed black
   peppercorns
3 bay leaves
1 tsp cloves
1 tsp whole allspice
1 10-cm cinammon stick
150 ml red wine vinegar
150 ml full-bodied
   Italian red wine
100 g sugar
100 ml water
2-3 Tbsp honey

1 Heat olive oil in a saucepot and sauté the onions and spices until soft but without colouring. This should take about 7–10 minutes.

2 Add the vinegar and wine and reduce until about a third remains, then add the sugar and water. Simmer the mixture until it thickens and becomes glossy. Pour in the honey and simmer for 2 minutes.

3 Cool and keep in sterilised glass jars or freeze for up to 3 months. This red onion jam goes well with red meat and is a great condiment on any antipasto platter.

chicken salad with comté cheese and du puy lentils

 15 min    serves 6

2 smoked chicken breasts, or half a roast chicken

2 shallots, finely sliced

6 sliced cornichons

50 ml smooth french dressing (*recipe on opposite page*)

oak leaf and frisée lettuce

150 g cooked du puy lentils (*recipe below*)

100 g comté or gruyère cheese

1 Slice the chicken breasts or roast chicken thinly and mix with sliced shallots and cornichons. Dress with half of the dressing.

2 Mix the lettuce with lentils and remaining dressing in a large bowl, shave the cheese into the bowl and gently mix to coat the leaves evenly.

3 To serve, lift the lettuce and chicken out of the bowl on to a plate and drizzle the du Puy lentils around the salad. A great and simple salad that's filling and tasty.

french du puy lentils

15 min   serves 6

200 g du puy lentils

1 medium-sized onion

1 small carrot

1 celery stalk

1 leek, white part only

100 g beef or wagyu bacon, optional (*recipe on page 86*)

50 ml extra virgin olive oil

4 bay leaves

fresh or dried thyme to taste

600 ml chicken stock or water

1 Cut all the vegetables and bacon, if using, into cubes the size of the lentils. Heat the olive oil in a pot over medium heat and sauté the vegetables for a couple of minutes. Add the lentils and herbs.

2 Stir to coat the lentils and release the flavour of the herbs, then add the chicken stock and simmer the lentils until tender but not broken.

notes

Season the lentils only after they are cooked as salt will make them hard to cook.

smooth french dressing with dijon mustard

100 ml sunflower oil

100 ml aged red wine vinegar

200 ml mild extra virgin
    olive oil

2 Tbsp dijon mustard

1 Tbsp english parsley,
    finely chopped

1 tsp chopped garlic

sea salt and freshly ground
    white pepper to taste

1 Pour all ingredients into a blender and blend until smooth. Do not strain the dressing.

2 Keep refrigerated and shake well before using.

organic pear chutney

1 .5 hr   makes 1.5 kg chutney

3 medium-sized yellow onions,
  cut into small cubes

500 g organic pink kiss apples,
  cut into small cubes

1 kg organic beurre bosc pears,
  cut into small cubes

100 ml cider vinegar

100 g organic brown sugar

200 ml water

30 g dried prunes

30 g dried apricot

30 g dried dates

3 bay leaves

½ Tbsp crushed black
  peppercorns

1 Tbsp black mustard seeds

½ tsp cloves

½ tsp crushed green cardamom

pinch of chilli flakes

1 Place everything in a large pot and cook over medium heat for an hour until it is thick and the fruits are soft but not broken into mash.

2 Store in sterilised glass jars. The chutney also freezes very well. In addition to pairing it with the terrine, I would serve this chutney with any roast meat, be it duck, turkey, chicken, beef or lamb. It is great on crusty bread with slices of cold cuts or cheese.

duck and foie gras terrine

1hr to cook
+ 1 hr to cool   serves 10

1.5 kg duck breast, minced

15 g nitrate salt

2 g ground white pepper

3 g sea salt

3 g pink peppercorns

15 g chopped garlic

100 g truffle, brunoised
   or finely diced

50 g plain flour

1 Tbsp chopped fresh thyme

1 Tbsp chopped parsley

50 g smoked duck or chicken
   breast, brunoised or finely
   diced

3 whole eggs

50 ml cognac

120 g foie gras, optional

1 Mix everything together and pour into a terrine mould lined with parchment paper.

2 Cook in a bain-marie in the oven at 150°C for 50 minutes.

3 Once cooked, remove from the bain-marie and place a weight on top of the terrine to press it flat.

4 Allow to cool and set in the refrigerator and slice when cold. Enjoy with organic pear chutney (*see opposite page*) and crusty bread.

seared foie gras, poached quince and hazelnut espuma

15 min + quince prepared 4 hr in advance   serves 6

foie gras

500 g raw foie gras
sea salt and ground
    white pepper
2 Tbsp cocoa butter

1 Slice the foie gras into 12 slices. Season both sides with salt and white pepper and coat with cocoa butter.

2 Heat a frying pan over high heat and very quickly sear four slices of foie gras at a time in the dry pan. Some fat will melt and cooking a few slices at a time will ensure the foie gras is brown on the outside and soft on the inside.

poached quince

2 litres water
500 g white sugar
1 cinnamon stick
1 vanilla bean
1 Tbsp black peppercorns
3 bay leaves
1 lemon, zest peeled off with
    a peeler
1 star anise
2 kg quince, peeled, cut in
    quarters and core removed –
    an alternative would be
    green guava or firm pears
fresh rosemary

1 Pre-heat your oven to 120°C.

2 Bring water, sugar and spices to a boil. Place the quince in an ovenproof dish and pour the hot syrup over to cover.

3 Lay a sheet of baking paper and aluminum foil on the quince and bake at 120°C for 3-4 hours.

4 When the quince is cooked, it will have changed from its raw yellow hue to a dark pink or even rich red colour depending on the level of natural sugars caramelising in the fruit.

5 Store in sterilised glass jars.

hazelnut espuma

100 g ground hazelnuts
50 g butter
250 ml milk
500 g cream
salt and ground pepper
1 Tbsp cornflour

1 Heat a saucepot over low to medium heat and melt the butter. Add hazelnuts and cook for 3-4 minutes.

2 When fragrant, add the milk and cream, season with salt and pepper and simmer the mixture for 2-3 minutes.

3 Add the cornflour and blend with a stab blender for 1 minute until thick and creamy.

4 Strain the mixture and pour into a siphon, charge with one N_2O gas cartridge and shake the bottle for 20 seconds.

5 Keep the bottle warm at 60°C until needed.

balsamic gastrique

100 ml balsamic vinegar
100 g white sugar

1 Mix the two ingredients in a saucepot and simmer for five minutes or until the sugar dissolves. Cool the liquid, then pour into a squeeze bottle and keep refrigerated.

To assemble

- Squeeze a circle of balsamic gastrique in the centre of the plate and dispense the hazelnut espuma inside this circle.

- Sauté the quince with a little fresh rosemary in olive oil until golden brown and caramelised, then place the quince on top of the espuma.

- Arrange two slices of foie gras on the quince and garnish the plate with some crushed hazelnuts and deep-fried leaves of rosemary.

Gravlax is something I make when I feel homesick; it's always comforting and a reminder of my roots.

gravlax

 30 min +
48 hr to cure

 serves 10-15

40 g salt
60 g sugar
1 kg salmon fillet
ground white pepper
50 g finely chopped dill

1 Mix the salt and sugar together and rub over the salmon fillet.

2 Season with white pepper and cover the fillet with the chopped dill.

3 I like to cure my gravlax for 36–48 hours. This way the texture is firmer and allows the brining and dill to work their magic.

sweet and hot mustard dressing

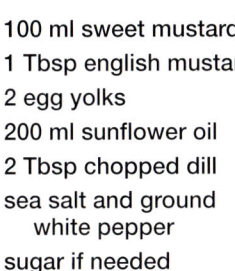 serves 10

100 ml sweet mustard
1 Tbsp english mustard
2 egg yolks
200 ml sunflower oil
2 Tbsp chopped dill
sea salt and ground
    white pepper
sugar if needed

1 Whisk together all ingredients and season to taste. The dressing should have a nice balance of sweetness and heat from the mustard.

2 Serve with gravlax as desired – topped on fish slices or on the side.

jellied calf's head with lobster and truffle

400 g cubes of veal head meat
  *(from jellied calf's head recipe
  on opposite page)*

1 whole poached lobster tail

40 g black truffle, finely sliced,
  then julienned into strips

chervil leaves

veal head poaching liquid

jellied calf's head

24 hr +
1 hr to cook

serves 6

1 calf's head, cut in half

white mirepoix (finely diced):

    4 leeks, white part only

    2 medium-sized yellow
      onions

    2 medium-sized parsnips

    1 medium-sized celeriac

    4 sticks celery

    2 heads garlic, cut in half
      horizontally

1 Tbsp white peppercorns

8 bay leaves

1 Soak the calf's head in ice water for 1 hour to clean out any blood and to firm the meat.

2 Place the calf's head in a stock-pot, pour lightly salted water to cover and bring to a boil.

3 Allow to simmer over low heat for 1 hour, then add the white mirepoix, white peppercorns and bay leaves.

4 Simmer for another hour, then remove from the heat and allow the meat to cool enough to handle. Reserve the poaching liquid.

5 Remove all visible meat from the head. Be careful with the brain and the muscles around the eyes and lips. Make sure you peel the tongue while it is still warm.

6 Cover the meat with the poaching liquid and chill overnight in the fridge. Store the remaining poaching liquid for use when assembling the dish.

7 Cut the meat into cubes the following day. Reserve 400 g of cubed veal head meat for the dish.

To assemble

■ Fill cone-shaped moulds with the veal head meat, lobster meat, truffle and chervil. When the mould is full, pour in the poaching liquid and leave to set in the fridge.

■ Once set, the jellied calf's head can easily be unmoulded and placed on a plate.

■ Serve with a piquant sauce, home-made mustard and pickled butternut pumpkin.

entrées

organic rye blinis with salmon rillette and poached egg

1.5 hr — **makes 15 blinis**

organic rye blinis

- 4 egg yolks
- 20 g dry yeast
- 1 tsp sugar
- 300 ml milk
- 130 g plain flour
- 130 g organic rye flour
- 6 egg whites

1 Mix the egg yolks with the yeast and 1 tsp sugar, heat the milk to slightly warmer than body temperature, pour over the egg yolks and stir to combine.

2 Whisk in the flours and place in a warm spot to proof for 45–60 minutes. When the batter is rising and bubbly, start whisking the egg whites to soft peaks. Gently fold in the egg whites and keep at room temperature before use.

3 To store, keep in the fridge overnight and when needed, place in a warm spot to proof again.

4 Pour into a ring mould and fry in a little butter. Turn the blini over when you can see the sides starting to cook.

salmon rillette

30 min **serves 4**

- 200 g fresh salmon
- 1 fennel bulb
- 2 Tbsp chopped dill
- 1 tsp salmon roe
- 100 g sour cream or crème fraiche

1 Lightly pan-fry or steam the salmon until 80% cooked. Let it cool down in the fridge.

2 Slice the fennel very thinly and blanch to remove the raw taste.

3 Flake the salmon and mix with fennel, dill, salmon roe and sour cream.

poached egg in cling film

10 min **serves 1**

- olive oil
- chopped chives
- salt and ground pepper
- 1 fresh egg

1 Place a sheet of cling film in a small bowl with about 10 cm overhang. Pour in a little olive oil, chopped chives, salt and ground pepper.

2 Break the egg on top of the chives and put some more oil, chives and seasoning on the egg.

3 Wrap the egg in the cling film and poach in simmering water for 5-6 minutes.

To serve

■ Serve the blini topped with salmon rillette and the poached egg.

beetroot with soft goat's curd filling, pine nut dressing and fine leaf salad

1 hr serves 6

organic beetroot "ravioli"

1 whole large beetroot
25 g butter
200 g goat's curd, or soft goat cheese
2 Tbsp chopped basil
1 lemon, grated zest only, no juice
30 ml extra virgin olive oil
salt and ground black pepper

1 Peel and slice the beetroot as thinly as possible to no thicker than 2 mm for a nice eating quality texture.

2 Melt the butter in a pot of lightly salted boiling water and put the beetroot in to cook for 15 seconds. Remove and cool in ice water.

3 Whisk the goat's curd, the chopped basil, lemon zest and extra virgin olive oil, and season with salt and black pepper.

4 Place a slice of beetroot on a tray with 1 tsp of goat's curd mixture in the centre, then top with another slice of beetroot and your "ravioli" is ready.

pine nut dressing

100 g pine nuts
100 ml extra virgin olive oil
salt and black pepper

1 Place pine nuts and oil in a blender and purée until smooth. Season to taste.

fine leaf salad

mixed lettuce
balsamic vinegar
crushed pine nuts

To serve

■ Arrange 3 "ravioli" on a plate around the lettuce, drizzle the pine nut dressing and a little vinegar over the salad, then sprinkle some crushed pine nuts around the dish.

oyster dressings

kilpatrick style

20 min · serves 24 oysters

1 whole smoked duck breast
2 whole shallots
1 bottle of 300 g heinz
    tomato sauce
2 Tbsp lea & perrins
    worcestershire sauce
½ tsp tabasco sauce

1 Cut duck breast and shallots into small brunoise (cubes 3×3 mm). Sauté in a little oil, leave to cool. Mix with sauces and taste to see if the balance is right for you. Shuck your fresh oysters and put a spoonful of Kilpatrick dressing on top and bake under a hot grill until caramelised. Eat while hot but don't burn yourself on the hot oyster shell.

mignonette

15 min   serves 10

1 Tbsp toasted black
    peppercorns
1 Tbsp toasted white
    peppercorns
4 Tbsp finely chopped shallots
200 ml good quality red
    wine vinegar

1 Make sure you toast the peppercorns until they are fragrant, then crush in a mortar and pestle.

2 Mix everything together and keep chilled. I like the aromatic spiciness of the toasted peppercorns in this classic oyster dressing.

lemon vodka snow

12 hr   serves 15-20

1 litre water
50 g sugar
50 ml lemon-infused vodka
2 Tbsp lemon juice

1 Blend all together and freeze in a Pacojet container, churn once frozen. Use a fork to fluff up the vodka "snow".

sea foam

15 min   serves 10

100 ml mineral water
2 Tbsp oyster juice
50 ml champagne
1 g lecite (*see glossary under
    texturas products, page 176*)

1 Place all ingredients in a tall narrow container and use a hand blender to create a foam the texture of frothed milk.

pickled cucumber and lime

15 min   serves 10

1 Tbsp lime juice
1 Tbsp champagne vinegar
1 tsp icing sugar
100 ml cucumber juice

1 Place the lime juice, vinegar and icing sugar in a bowl. Juice the cucumber straight into this bowl to preserve its vibrant green colour.

sweet garlic butter

30 min   serves 10

500 g soft butter
100 g chopped garlic
2 Tbsp chopped garlic chives
grated zest of 1 lemon
sugar syrup
ground white pepper to taste

1 Whip butter, garlic, garlic chives and lemon zest until pale and creamy. Season with sugar syrup and a little white pepper.

2 Place a dollop of garlic butter on top of fresh oysters.

3 Bake under a hot grill for 2-3 minutes until the oysters are cooked and butter starts to caramelise.

champagne and vodka fried

15 min   serves 15

100 g rice flour
100 g flour
75 ml vodka
1 tsp baking powder
150 ml champagne

1 Mix all ingredients together to a smooth batter. Add the champagne last to keep as many bubbles as possible.

2 Pour quickly into a soda siphon and charge with a soda cartridge. Refrigerate.

3 Dust oysters with rice flour then spray the batter over the oyster and fry in hot oil.

smoked jade
tiger abalone salad 1 hr  serves 4

30 ml peanut oil
100 g oyster mushrooms
2 sliced shallots
1 tsp sugar
small pinch of chilli flakes
1 Tbsp dark soya sauce
1 Tbsp light soya sauce
4 cooked jade tiger abalones
woodchips to smoke the
    abalones
120 g washed baby spinach
    leaves

1 First of all, heat a wok or a frying pan with the peanut oil until very hot and add the oyster mushrooms.

2 Fry the mushrooms until they have a nice golden brown colour and are starting to crisp up. Lower the heat and add the shallots, fry for a couple of minutes then add sugar and chili. Caramelise the sugar, then add sauces and cook until evenly coated and the mushrooms are shiny.

3 Remove from the wok and leave to cool.

4 For the smoked abalones, place the woodchips in a wok and heat over low heat. Arrange abalones on a rack on top of the wok and wrap the rack in aluminium foil to avoid any smoke escaping.

5 Leave the wok over a low flame and smoke the abalones for 20 minutes.

6 Slice each abalone into 6 slices and mix with mushrooms and baby spinach. Drizzle with a little olive oil and serve garnished with some crispy salsify and chive flowers.

potato terrine

2 hr   serves 10

1 kg chat potatoes
50 g dill
knob of butter
3 red onions
5-7 spring onion
25 g chives
400 g sour cream or
    crème fraiche
salt and ground white pepper
6 hard-boiled eggs
400 g smoked salmon slices
    (optional)
salad leaves
red radishes
celery
cucumber

1 Boil the chat potatoes in their skins in salted water with dill stems and a small knob of butter, then let the potatoes cool down completely in the fridge (this can be done 1 day in advance).

2 Dice the red onions into fine cubes, slice the spring onions and chives finely and chop the dill tips.

3 Mix the sour cream or crème fraiche with the onions and herbs. Season with salt and white pepper.

4 Slice the eggs into thin slices.

5 When the potatoes have cooled, crush them with your hands to release the starch and make it creamy, stir in the sour cream mix and mix well.

6 In a loaf tin or cake mould, layer the potato mix with the smoked salmon slices and sliced eggs.

7 Make sure that you have a layer of potato on the bottom and the top.

8 Make a salad of the salad leaves, red radishes, celery and cucumber and arrange on top of the potato terrine.

twice-baked alaskan king crab soufflé

1 hr

makes
6-8 soufflés

150 g flour
150 g butter
600 ml milk
3 egg yolks
4 egg whites
150 g cooked and picked
    alaskan king crab meat
ground white pepper
500 ml cream, when serving

1 Pre-heat your oven to 160°C then start by cooking the butter and flour to a blonde roux, add the milk and boil for 20 minutes, whisking all the time – the mix will be very thick!

2 Let the mix cool a little, but while still hot, add the egg yolks one by one followed by the crab meat and

season with white pepper. Whisk the egg whites to stiff peaks and fold into the soufflé base. Butter Chinese teacups and pour the mix into these.

3 Bake in a water bath at 160°C for 20 minutes and allow to cool slightly in the mould before you unmould onto baking paper.

To serve

■ When serving place the soufflé in a baking dish and pour in enough cream to come one third up the side of the soufflé. Bake at 180°C for 15-17 minutes until the cream has been absorbed and the soufflé looks nice and golden brown.

Smoking Allowed. This has become my signature dish over the years. It is a modern interpretation of smoked salmon. Being Swedish, I love Nordic flavours and I grew up learning to prepare this traditional dish. My early culinary career in Australia also influenced my interpretation of this dish. I use the very best ocean trout instead of salmon because this gives me a fish that is rich and flavourful but with a nice clean taste, rather than an overly fatty flavour. Salmon's texture cannot compare with the Petuna ocean trout's. When smoked, the fish flakes beautifully and still keeps its shiny raw look.

Presenting **Smoking Allowed** in a creative and eye-catching style is always a challenging but satisfying experience. Smoking the fish in front of my guests gives this dish the dramatic touch it needs. The salt and river stones are only for presentation and can be varied with burnt woodchips, seashells, seaweed, clam shells and mussel shells to suit the occasion.
At times I use this "table-side smoking" method when serving wood pigeons.
I fill a jar with dried leaves, mushrooms and even a truffle if the season allows, just to give that forest feeling and right aroma. The possibilities are endless... hmm, maybe we could do a...

ocean trout – sous-vide

600 g ocean trout fillet

2 tbsp gravlax mix,
(2 parts sugar +
1.5 parts fine salt)

2 tsp dill, finely chopped

a pinch of white pepper

vacuum pac bag

1 Season the fish with gravlax mixture, chopped dill and white pepper.

2 Put the fish in a vacuum bag and seal to 100 percent, cook for 20 minutes at 43°C.

3 After 20 minutes, place the fish in ice water and allow to cool.

4 If you do not have access to a vacuum pack machine, you can bake the ocean trout fillet in an oven set at 60°C, until the internal temperature of the fish is 43°C.

pickled cucumber

1 small cucumber

1 tsp gravlax mix (2 parts sugar
+ 1.5 parts fine salt)

1 tsp chopped dill

1 tsp champagne vinegar

1 Using a peeler, slice long strips of the cucumber and combine with the gravlax mixture. Leave for 10 minutes, then rinse under cold water. Dry on paper towel and add the chopped dill and champagne vinegar. Eat it straightaway as it loses its bright green colour the longer it is kept.

swedish style mustard

150 ml yellow mustard seeds

50 ml brown mustard seeds

4 Tbsp red wine vinegar

4 Tbsp sugar syrup

200 ml water

100 ml grapeseed oil

1 tsp turmeric powder

1 tsp english mustard powder

salt and ground white pepper

1 Soak the mustard seeds in just enough water to cover. Leave to soak at room temperature overnight. Place the mustard seeds in a blender, add the vinegar and syrup. Blend into a rough paste, then slowly drizzle in the oil. If it gets a little thick, add more water. When all the oil is incorporated, add the turmeric, English mustard powder and season with salt and pepper to taste. Keep the mustard in clean and sterilised jars and leave for one week before using.

pressed potato salad

500 g new season potatoes
50 g dill
knob of butter
3 medium shallots
3 spring onions
25 g chives
200 g sour cream or
    crème fraiche
salt and ground white pepper

1 Boil the new season potatoes in their skins in salted water with dill stems and a small knob of butter. Let the potatoes cool down completely in the fridge (this can be done one day in advance). Cut the shallots into fine cubes, slice the spring onions and chives finely, chop the dill tops. Mix the sour cream or crème fraiche with the spring onions and herbs, season with salt and white pepper. When the potatoes have cooled, crush them with your hands to release the starch and make it creamy, stir in the sour cream mix and mix well. Using a 5-cm ring mould, press the potatoes into a perfect cylinder 3-cm high.

Presentation:

ocean trout roe
cucumber cress
2 Tbsp woodchips

- Arrange the pickled cucumber strips on a plate and the ocean trout portions on top.

- To the right of the ocean trout, place a pressed potato salad cylinder, drizzle the mustard on the plate and garnish with ocean trout roe and cucumber cress.

- Heat two tablespoons of woodchips in a wok and place a wine glass turned upside down over the woodchips to catch the smoke. Place the wine glass over the ocean trout in order to smoke it and bring the plate to the table and lift the wine glass in front of your friends.

I describe this dish as typical Australian vineyard cuisine. It is so hard to explain what Australian cuisine is. For me it's an

unwritten rule of mixing ingredients and cultures, using the freshest seasonal produce to create clean, fresh flavours.

seared scallops with roasted beetroot purée and grilled goat cheese

1.5 hr   serves 10

12 large scallops
4 slices goat cheese
beetroot purée (*recipe follows*)
salad leaves like frisée
   and red chard
extra virgin olive oil
red wine vinegar

1 Season and sear the scallops over high heat in a little olive oil, grill the goat cheese under a hot grill and place in the centre of a dinner plate.

2 Make a large circle around the cheese with the beetroot purée, building layer by layer.

3 Dress the salad leaves with extra virgin olive oil and red wine vinegar. Arrange a pile of dressed leaves over cheese.

4 Arrange the scallops on the beetroot purée around the salad.

roasted beetroot purée

400 g beetroots
75 ml extra virgin olive oil
3 tsp red wine vinegar
sea salt and ground black pepper

1 Wash the beetroots but do not peel them.

2 Coat with oil and season. Roast at 180°C for 1 hour or until soft. While beetroots are still warm, peel and place in a blender. Blend until smooth and add oil, vinegar and sea salt and black pepper to taste.

This recipe uses Southern Ocean Blue Fin Tuna because it's sustainably caught in the clear cold waters off South Australia.

tuna salad 🕐 1 hr 🥄 serves 6

tuna

480 g southern ocean
   blue fin tuna
salt and ground black pepper
   to taste
60 ml (4 Tbsp) dark soya sauce
60 ml (4 Tbsp) peanut oil

1 Marinate tuna with salt, pepper and soya sauce for 20 minutes. While tuna marinates, prepare a tray with ice cubes, and layer aluminum foil on top. Heat up peanut oil in a non-stick frying pan until hot and smoking. Sear the tuna, for approximately 7 seconds each side. Place the tuna in the tray with ice and aluminium foil. Allow to cool for 1 hour.

2 While the tuna is cooling down, make the tomato jelly and Parmesan crisps (*see next page*).

tomato jelly

1 kg red and ripe roma tomatoes

40 ml simple sugar syrup, ratio of sugar to water is 1:1 (e.g. 1 cup sugar dissolved in 1 cup water)

½ tsp sea salt

1 Tbsp ground black pepper

20 g tomato paste

½ tsp agar-agar powder

8 gelatine leaves

1 Blend Roma tomato, syrup, seasoning and tomato paste to a smooth purée.

2 Pour into a pot and bring to boil, add the agar-agar and boil for 2 minutes.

3 Add the gelatine leaves and stir until melted.

4 Strain and keep the pulp for later, then pour liquid into a 12-cm circle silicone mould. Leave to set in the chiller.

parmesan crisps

parmesan cheese
non-stick pan

1 Grate the Parmesan cheese on a microplane, into a cold non-stick pan.

2 Place pan over a medium heat, and cook Parmesan until it melts and bubbles.

3 Slide the crisps out onto a plate, leave to cool.

4 Break crisps into irregular shapes.

salad

12 large asparagus (peeled and cut into three)

3 courgettes or 1 zucchini (cut in half lengthwise)

1 aubergine (cut into finger-sized pieces)

extra virgin olive oil

salt and ground pepper

1 Brush the vegetables with extra virgin olive oil, salt and pepper.

2 Grill until tender.

roasted tomatoes

3 roma tomatoes
 (cut into quarters)
12 cherry tomatoes
 (cut into halves)
1 tsp of chopped thyme
1 tsp chopped garlic
extra virgin olive oil
salt and ground pepper

1 Mix all ingredients together.

2 Bake in oven at 160°C for 15 minutes.

3 Remove and allow to cool to room temperature.

dressing

50 g fresh basil
75 g sunflower oil

1 Bring water to boil in a pot. Quickly cook basil in water for 10 seconds.

2 Remove, dip in ice water and squeeze dry.

3 Place in blender, add sunflower oil, and blend until smooth.

4 Strain, and keep the green oil in the fridge.

garnish
**cucumber cress,
 a few leaves**

To serve

- Place the ring of tomato jelly on the plate.

- Arrange the vegetables creatively, with the asparagus spears standing up. Add a few leaves of cress amongst the vegetables.

- Slice the tuna into 1-cm thick slices and drape over the vegetables.

- Stand a few shards of Parmesan crisps around the vegetables and tuna.

- Make a quenelle, or egg-shaped dumpling, using a teaspoon, out of the tomato pulp reserved earlier.

- Drizzle basil oil over the dish and serve.

vegetarian noodle salad with soya beans, wakame and persimmon

30 min   serves 6

400 g fresh soba noodles
3 spring onions
40 g soaked soya beans
10 g wakame seaweed
2 Tbsp dark soya sauce
2 Tbsp light soya sauce
2 Tbsp honey
150 g cooked soba noodles
1 persimmon

1 Bring a pot of salted water to the boil and boil the fresh soba noodles for 3-4 minutes. Taste one to see that it is tender but still has a bite to it. Once cooked, strain and cool in ice water. Drain the soba noodles and keep in the refrigerator until needed.

2 Boil the soya beans with soya sauces, honey, spring onions, seaweed and water to cover, until soft and tender. Once cooked, remove the beans and glaze with a little more soya sauce and honey. Keep adding the cooking liquid to create a viscous and shiny sauce. Mix a little more seaweed and chopped spring onion into the soya beans.

3 Toss the soya beans with cooked soba noodles and twirl into a neat pile on a plate. Slice a ripe persimmon thinly to surround the soba noodles. Top the twirl with a few more soya beans and a little seaweed, glaze with the honey soya sauce, and sprinkle with spring onion and sesame seeds.

"fake" scallops baked with green chilli, garlic and lime

30 min · serves 6

600 ml unsweetened soya bean milk
4 whole eggs
finely chopped spring onion whites
salt and ground white pepper

1 Pour the soya bean milk and eggs into a container and blend until perfectly smooth.

2 Strain into a baking tray, sprinkle with spring onion whites and season with salt and pepper.

3 Steam the mixture for 15 minutes until set. Allow to cool then cut into large circles resembling the shape of scallop meat.

marinade

2 large green chillies
3 garlic cloves
2 shallots
1 lime, zested and juiced
4 Tbsp extra virgin olive oil

1 Finely chop the aromatics and mix with the lime and olive oil. Season with salt and pepper.

2 Lay the "fake" scallops in scallop shells and add 1 Tbsp marinade on top and bake for 2 minutes under a hot grill.

soups

"Texture is very important in my soups. You will find that almost all my soups have their fillings and garnishes cooked separately."

beef and whisky consommé

4 + 2hr   serves 12

2 kg beef neck bone

1.5 kg oxtail

1 kg beef shin, cut like osso buco

mirepoix (finely diced):

   500 g peeled onion.

   500 g carrot

   500 g leek

   4 celery sticks

   3 heads garlic

20 bay leaves

2 Tbsp dry thyme

small bunch thyme

2 Tbsp black peppercorns

150 ml whisky

1 Cut all the beef into slices or large chunks. Roast for 30 minutes at 220°C, then turn the pieces over and roast for another 15-20 minutes. Pour off all the fat before you put the beef in the stockpot. Roast the vegetable mirepoix the same way until evenly brown. Cover the beef with cold water and bring to boil.

2 Skim thoroughly; allow to simmer for 3-4 hours before adding the vegetables and herbs. Simmer the stock for a total of 5 hours, then strain through a fine strainer and reduce slowly until 2-3 litres remain. Chill the stock overnight.

to clarify beef consommé

2-3 litres beef stock

mirepoix (finely diced):
    1 peeled onion
    2 carrot
    1 leek
    1 celery stick

clarification raft:
    **500g fresh lean beef,
       like knuckle or rump**
    3-4 egg whites
    1 tsp fresh thyme

salt and ground white pepper

1 Melt the cold jellied stock (the stock cannot be warm but must be melted). Blend the mirepoix in a kitchen blender until finely chopped. Blend the beef to a rough paste then add the thyme, egg whites and quickly blend together to a form a loose paste.

2 Mix the beef and mirepoix together, season well, add to the stock and stir it in using your hand to feel that there are no lumps. Place the pot on medium heat and bring to simmer, keep stirring the stock to avoid the meat sticking to the bottom of the pot. The clarification raft will float when the consommé is ready. Carefully ladle out the clear broth and keep chilled until needed. The raft is to be discarded once the soup is ladled out. If you try to take out the raft first, rather than the broth, you are likely to break the raft and it will make the consommé cloudy.

tofu noodle
15 min   serves 10

200 g silken tofu
200 ml water
**12 g metil (*see glossary under
    texturas products, page 176*)**
3 Tbsp white truffle oil

1 Place tofu and water in a blender and blend until smooth. Keep the engine running, add the metil and truffle oil. Let the engine run for 60 seconds then strain the mixture and chill to 4°C. Once cold, put into a squeeze bottle and extract into hot, clear beef consommé.

cream of escargot soup

1hr   serves 6

2 dozens escargot
1 large onion
4 cloves of garlic
1 leek, white part only
50 g butter
sea salt and ground white
   pepper
50 g flour
70 ml white wine
1 litre chicken stock
2 Tbsp chopped parsley

1 Cut the escargot in half and clean off any shell or sand in the centre cavity. Chop the onion and garlic finely and slice the leek into thin slices.

2 Melt the butter in a pot and add vegetables and escargot. Season with salt and pepper. Cook over a medium heat until the onions are soft, about 3-4 minutes.

3 Add flour and use a whisk to stir out any lumps. Pour in white wine and chicken stock, whisk until the soup comes to boil, then simmer for 20 minutes. Use a hand-held blender to blitz the escargot in the soup. When serving, add the chopped parsley and taste if more salt and pepper is needed.

escargot and garlic butter croquettes

20 min   serves 6

1 dozen escargot
75 g sweet garlic butter
3 Tbsp flour
1 whole egg
6 Tbsp panko
   breadcrumbs
cooking oil

1 Cut the escargot in half and clean off any shell or sand in the centre cavity.

2 Coat two escargot halves with garlic butter, then roll in flour, egg and panko to create a crispy coating.

3 Fry the escargot in hot oil before serving. Use to garnish cream of escargot soup.

smooth
chicken soup

4 hr   serves 8

chicken stock

2 kg chicken bones
2 kg chicken wings
3 litres water

1 Wash bones and wings in cold water. Place in a pot and cover with fresh water.

2 Bring to boil and boil rapidly for 1 hour. Strain the mix and set the bones aside to cool.

3 Separate the bones from the meat. Add the meat back into the pot and boil for another 1 hour.

4 Strain and keep the stock warm.

100 g skinless chicken breast
750 g red onion
butter
600 g cream
salt and ground white pepper

1 Poach the chicken breast in the chicken stock. Remove the chicken breast when cooked and cooled.

2 Cut the red onion and chicken breast into cubes and sauté in butter, then add the chicken stock and reduce to 1.2 litres. Add cream and season with salt and white pepper.

3 Strain the soup, thicken with a little wheat starch if needed and strain again.

Garnish

■ 4 confit shallots, cut in half and seared to colour.

■ 8 cooked morel mushrooms

■ 2 Tbsp grated Parmesan cheese

■ Freshly picked thyme leaves

■ 20 small sourdough croutons

soups

crab soup with spicy crabmeat omelette

1 hr   serves 6

1 kg fresh swimmer crabs

1 medium onion

2 stalks leek

300 g yellow capsicum, deseeded

300 g red capsicum, deseeded

2 stalks lemongrass

3 deseeded red chilies

1 thumb-size piece of ginger

75 ml olive oil

250 ml white wine

500 g canned san marzano tomatoes

salt and ground white pepper

1 Clean the crabs by removing the gills under the shell. Do not wash away any of the insides. Cut all the vegetables into small cubes about 1-cm each. Slice the lemongrass, red chilli and ginger into thin slices. Heat the olive oil in a large pot and sauté the lemongrass, red chilli and ginger until fragrant. Add onion, leek and capsicum. Cook for 2-3 minutes. While cooking, cut the crabs into smaller pieces and keep all the juices.

2 Add the crab to the pot and sauté until it turns red and the juices have reduced by half. Pour in white wine and reduce by half, then add tomatoes and cover with a lid. Simmer the soup for 30 minutes. Allow the soup to cool slightly, then transfer to a blender and blend until very smooth, shells and all. This will give you maximum flavour and the right texture. Strain the soup through a fine strainer, season with salt and white pepper and maybe a little cream for added richness. Serve the soup with fresh crabmeat omelette garnished with watercress.

spicy crabmeat omelette

15 min   serves 6

6 fresh eggs
salt and ground white pepper
pinch of chilli flakes
2 spring onions
1 lemon
150 g picked crabmeat
15 g butter

1 Crack the eggs into a bowl and season with salt, pepper and chilli flakes. Slice the spring onions into thin rings, grate the zest of the lemon and mix with the beaten eggs. Add the crabmeat to the egg mixture.

2 Heat the butter and when it's just melted, pour in half the egg mixture and cook while stirring lightly. Once the egg starts to set, start folding your omelette and cook it just enough so it is still soft and creamy in the centre. Transfer to a plate and repeat with the remaining mixture. Slice the omelette and divide between your soup bowls. Pour in the hot crab soup and garnish with watercress.

french onion soup

1 hr   serves 4

8 large yellow onions
4 cloves garlic
50 ml olive oil
2 tsp dried thyme
6 bay leaves
500 ml full-bodied red wine
1 litre chicken stock
sea salt and ground white
　　pepper

1 Peel and slice the onions thinly. Chop the garlic and mix with the sliced onions. Add a little olive oil in a pot and sauté the onions and garlic until soft but without taking on any colour. Season with sea salt and ground white pepper, add thyme and bay leaves.

2 Pour in the red wine and reduce by two-thirds then add the chicken stock and simmer the soup for 20 minutes. Serve with crusty bread and butter. Adding croutons and grated Comté or Parmesan cheese would be a nice touch.

jerusalem artichoke and
scallop skirt soup ⏱ 🥄

1 hr   serves 4

soup

200 g jerusalem artichokes,
   peeled and kept in ice water

scallop skirts from 12 fresh scallops
   (skirts are the flesh attached to the
   scallop meat)

4 shallots, finely chopped

½ vanilla bean, cut open
   and seeds scraped out

400 ml chicken stock

30 g butter

50 g double cream, 48 percent

1 Prepare the soup. Place all
ingredients in a saucepot and bring
to boil. Allow to simmer until the
artichokes are soft.

2 Pour everything into a blender
and blend until very smooth. Strain
and season with salt and pepper.

harvey bay scallops

salt and ground white pepper

extra virgin olive oil

1 Season scallops and sear them
in olive oil just before serving, then
place in the soup bowl.

vanilla oil

75 ml extra virgin olive oil

½ vanilla bean, cut open
   and seeds scraped out

1 Mix oil with the half vanilla bean
and heat to 75°C. Keep at this
temperature for 10 minutes in order
for the vanilla to release its flavour
and aroma. Drizzle the vanilla oil
over the soup when serving.

mushroom soup

 2 hr   serves 8

1 kg button mushroom, sliced
4 portobello mushrooms, sliced
50 g butter
50 ml olive oil
2 onions, cut into 1 cm dice
10 cloves garlic, sliced
10 sprigs of fresh thyme
3 bay leaves
1.5 litres chicken stock
salt and ground black pepper
50 ml cream

1 Sauté mushrooms in butter and oil, making sure the mushrooms are a nice seared colour; this should take up to 30 minutes to make sure all water is evaporated from the mushrooms.

2 Add onions and garlic, more oil and butter if needed and keep sautéeing until soft. Add thyme, bay leaves and the chicken stock.

3 Boil until all ingredients are soft, then remove the thyme and bay leaves. Pour the soup into a blender and blend until very smooth. Strain if needed. Season with salt and black pepper.

4 Bring soup to boil. Add cream to taste.

Serving

- 25 g butter
- 10 french mushrooms
- 1 portobello mushroom, sliced
- 50 g shimeji mushrooms, separated from each other
- 1 tsp fresh thyme leaves
- 2 stalks spring onion, sliced green and white

Sauté above ingredients and arrange in soup bowls. Blend the soup with a hand blender to froth the top and ensure it is smooth and even.

My seafood soup started out like a French Bouillabaisse. I bought typical Mediterranean fish such as rascasse, rouget grondin, conger eel, dorade, monkfish and grey mullet. I would add crabs and mussels together with lots of saffron and Pernod. Over the years, I started to use the freshest seafood available locally instead of bringing them in from across the planet just to get a particular fish that can give the true flavour of a Bouillabaisse. Instead of serving the

fish that was cooked in my seafood soup, I blended it perfectly smooth to get a rich and viscous soup. Before serving my seafood soup, I cook a fresh fillet of fish, a Moreton Bay bug tail and a large scallop to add to it. I arrange these in the soup bowl with some caramelised onion, roasted Roma tomato and a saffron-infused cooked potato, just to put back a little of that Bouillabaisse flavour from which my seafood soup started out with.

my seafood soup 3 hr  serves 15-20

1.5 kg snapper
1.5 kg red mullet
1 kg freshwater eel
1 kg crabs
500 g clams
5 oranges
3 lemons
2 kg ripe tomatoes
2 kg fennel
1 kg onion
1 kg leek
1 kg carrot
200 g garlic
2 g saffron filaments
25 g fresh thyme
1 Tbsp white peppercorns
10 bay leaves
1 bottle (750 ml) white wine
1 kg tomato paste
cream
salt and ground pepper

1 Scale and gut all the fish and cut into large chunks. Crush the crabs and remove the gills. Shuck the clams. Peel the zest of the oranges and lemons, discarding the white pith. Cut the flesh into quarters and set aside.

2 Cut the remaining vegetables (tomatoes, fennel, onion, leek, carrot) into 3 x 3-cm dice.

3 In a large pot, start layering the fish heads, followed by the flesh of the fish, crabs and clams. Add the citrus, herbs and spices (garlic, saffron filament, thyme, peppercorn and bay leaves). Pour in a bottle of wine, then top with tomato paste and the remaining vegetables.

4 Add enough cold water to cover the vegetables, bring to boil over a medium heat. Skim the soup and remove scum on the surface. Let the soup simmer for 2 hours, then transfer everything to a blender and blend until very smooth.

5 Strain the soup through a fine strainer. Serve the soup with a little cream and salt and pepper to bring out the flavours.

pumpkin and perrier soup

1 hr serves 8-10

2 kg butternut pumpkin,
   organic if possible

750 ml perrier water

100 g butter

2 Tbsp sea salt

25 white peppercorns,
   tied in a cloth bag

1 Cut the pumpkin in half and remove the seeds. Peel the pumpkin until all the skin and yellow flesh are removed. Using only the most orange flesh of the pumpkin will give you the best result for this soup.

2 Cut the pumpkins into 3-cm chunks and place in a pot, then pour over just enough Perrier water to cover. Add the butter and the 2 tablespoons sea salt and white peppercorns.

3 Cover the pot and bring to boil and simmer until the pumpkin is soft and translucent. Remove the cloth bag, then blend the soup until very smooth. Serve the soup with seared scallops and a drizzle of vanilla oil (*see page 62*).

sweetcorn and basil soup with ricotta cheese

30 min · serves 8

8 fresh sweetcorn
50 ml olive oil
30 g butter
2 onions, peeled and chopped
2 leeks, stem sliced
   into 5-mm thick slices
salt and black pepper
2 litres chicken stock
50 g basil (stalks and leaves)
sea salt and ground white
   pepper
200 g ricotta cheese
cream (optional)

1 Cut the corn off the cob, and reserve the cobs. Heat the olive oil and the butter in a large pot over medium heat. Add onion and leek.

2 Cook for 1 minute, then add the corn kernels and cook for 2 minutes. Season with salt and pepper, then add the chicken stock and the corn cobs.

3 Pick all the leaves off the 50 g of basil and keep to one side. Add the basil stems to the soup. Let the soup simmer for 20 minutes, then

remove from heat and cool to room temperature.

4 Blend the soup with two-thirds of the basil leaves, then strain the soup. Finely chop the remaining basil leaves, mix with the ricotta cheese, then add salt and black pepper to taste.

5 When serving, heat the soup and add some cream if desired. Spoon the ricotta cheese into the soup bowl and pour the hot soup on top.

beef

> "I can talk about beef until the cows come home, I have been told. I have a great passion for beef and its potential."

Diamantina beef cattle (named after the Diamantina River that flows through Central Queensland) are bred in the Gulf of Carpentaria, arguably one of Australia's best pastoral regions.

beef rib with soft polenta

4 hr   serves 4

1 kg beef short ribs

1 carrot cut into 2-cm slices

1 onion cut into 2-cm slices

1 stalk of leek, cut into
   2-cm slices

1 stalk of celery cut into
   2-cm slices

1 bulb of garlic cut in half

1 Tbsp dried thyme

4 bay leaves

500 ml full-bodied red wine,
   a barossa valley shiraz
   or merlot

extra virgin olive oil

salt and ground pepper

beef stock or water to cover

1 Pre-heat your oven to 160°C. Season the beef ribs with salt and pepper and sear in a large frying pan with a little olive oil. Turn the ribs over when they are brown and caramelised; this will take a few minutes.

2 Remove the ribs from the pan and add the vegetables, keep cooking until the vegetables are evenly coloured. Add the herbs and pour in the red wine and reduce by half.

3 Place the beef ribs in an ovenproof dish and pour the vegetables on top, then top up with beef stock or water to cover. Cover the dish with baking paper then aluminum foil and cook in the oven for about 3 hours. The ribs are ready when a knife cuts through it like butter and the meat falls off the bone. When serving, drizzle some of the cooking liquid over the ribs and heat under the grill in your oven. Keep basting with more cooking liquid for a nice sticky glaze.

fragrant polenta

20 min   serves 4

1 onion

500 ml milk

100 ml water

1 leek, white part only

3 cloves garlic

1 sprig of rosemary

1 small bunch fresh thyme

2 bay leaves

100 g fine polenta

2 Tbsp chopped fresh basil

50 g grated parmesan cheese

sea salt and ground white
   pepper

1 Finely slice the onion and crush the herbs in a mortar and pestle. Heat the milk, water, onion and herbs, and simmer the mixture for 10 minutes.

2 Season and strain the milk into another pot. Slowly pour in the polenta and whisk until the mix is smooth and keep cooking for 10 minutes. Add some water if the mixture seems too thick for your liking. When serving, add the chopped basil and grated cheese. Serve with slow-braised beef ribs glazed in their cooking jus.

bourguignon style beef cheeks

5 hr serves 6

3 whole beef cheeks,
about 400 g each

2 carrots cut into 2-cm slices

2 onions cut into 2-cm slices

2 stalks of leek, cut into
2-cm slices

2 stalks of celery cut into
2-cm slices

1 bulb of garlic cut in half

1 Tbsp dried thyme

4 bay leaves

500 ml full-bodied red wine,
a barossa valley shiraz or
merlot

extra virgin olive oil

salt and ground pepper

beef stock or water to cover

1 Pre-heat your oven to 160°C.

2 Season the beef cheeks with salt and pepper and sear in a large frying pan with a little olive oil. Turn the cheeks over when they are brown and caramelised; this will take a few minutes.

3 Remove the cheeks from the pan and add the vegetables, keep cooking until the vegetables are evenly coloured. Add the herbs and pour in the red wine and reduce by half.

4 Place the beef cheeks in an ovenproof dish, pour vegetables on top, then top up with beef stock or water to cover. Cover the dish with baking paper then aluminum foil and cook in the oven for 4-5 hours. The cheeks are ready when a knife cuts through them like butter.

5 The beef cheeks will be best eaten after they have cooled in the liquid and reheated the next day. Reserve beef stock for garnish (see below).

bourguignon garnish

30 mins serves 6

150 g smoked bacon,
from pork or beef

30 small button mushrooms

24 shallots, peeled and
kept whole

250ml full-bodied red wine,
a barossa valley shiraz or
merlot

1 litre beef stock from braising
the beef cheeks

potato purée with white
truffle oil

1 Sauté the bacon and mushrooms in a little olive oil, add the shallots and cook until they get a little colour. Pour over about three-quarters of a bottle of red wine and reduce by half. Add the reduced beef jus from braising the beef cheeks and cook until combined.

2 Just before serving, add the last quarter of red wine and cook for 5 minutes.

3 Serve with braised beef cheek and potato purée flavoured with white truffle oil.

tongue confit salad

30 min +
75.5 hr for
confit

serves 6

tongue confit

1 kg beef tongue
2 kg duck fat, to confit the tongue
salt brine:
   120 g fine salt
   1.5 litres water
   30 g nitrate salt or saltpetre
     (potassium nitrate), optional

1 Mix together the ingredients for the salt brine and soak the beef tongue in this for 72 hours in the fridge. Remove the tongue from the brine and rinse under running water for 10 minutes to remove excess salt. Place the tongue in a large pot and cover with the duck fat. Bring the pot to a slow simmer and cook for about 3 hours. Skim off any scum that rises to the surface during the cooking process.

salad

200 g tongue confit, thinly
   sliced
6 shallot, thinly sliced
12 cornichons, sliced into rings
10 sprigs flat leaf parsley
3 heads baby coz lettuce,
   roughly sliced

1 Mix all the ingredients for the salad in a large bowl.

mustard dressing

2 Tbsp dijon mustard
1 tsp english mustard
150 ml sunflower oil
50 ml champagne vinegar
sea salt and ground white
   pepper

1 Emulsify the mustard dressing and dress the tongue confit salad.

corned beef brisket with horseradish velouté

72 hr + 1 hr   serves 6

corned beef brisket

1.5 kg beef brisket or tri-tip
salt brine:
  240 g fine salt
  3 litres water
  60 g nitrate salt or saltpetre (potassium nitrate), optional
  water to cover by 5 cm
1 carrot
1 parsnip
2 onions
2 leeks
1 celeriac or celery
6 bay leaves
1 Tbsp white peppercorns
10 stalks parsley or 1 tsp dried parsley flakes

1 Trim the meat of any surface fat and sinew.

2 Mix together the ingredients for the salt brine and soak the beef in this for 72 hours in the fridge.

3 Remove the beef from the brine and rinse under running water for 10 minutes to remove excess salt.

4 Place the beef in a large pot, cut all the vegetables into 3 x 3-cm cubes and place on top of the beef. Add the spices and cover with cold water.

5 Bring the pot to boil and reduce to a slow simmer for about 3 hours.

6 Skim off any scum that rises to the surface during the cooking process. Reserve cooking liquid for horseradish velouté (*recipe on next page*).

horseradish velouté

100 g unsalted butter
100 g plain flour
2 litres cooking liquid from
 corned beef
50 g horseradish, freshly grated
250 g cream
½ tsp ground white pepper

1 Heat the butter over medium heat and once melted add the flour, stir with a whisk and cook for 2-3 minutes.

2 Pour in the cooking liquid and whisk until smooth and thick. Keep stirring the sauce and cook it for 15-20 minutes. Strain and add some fresh horseradish and a little cream and white pepper if desired

michael's mexican

1.5 hr   serves 6-8

500 g minced beef
4 Tbsp mexican spice mix
1 Tbsp paprika powder
1 Tbsp dried oregano
1 tsp cayenne pepper
2 onions, finely chopped
4 cloves garlic,
 finely chopped
2 red capsicums, cut into
 5 x 5-mm dice
1 red chilli, finely chopped
5 button mushrooms,
 finely chopped
2-3 cobs of corns,
 kernels removed
1 can cannellini beans,
 lima beans or baked beans
1 can red kidney beans
2 cans crushed tomatoes
sunflower oil
salt and ground pepper

1 In a large pot with a little sunflower oil, sauté all the meat until it takes on a nice brown and caramelised colour. Add half the spices and cook for a few minutes until fragrant.

2 Remove the meat from the pot and keep aside. Add a little more oil to the pot and sauté the vegetables until transparent, then add the other half of the spices and cook for a few minutes.

3 Add the minced meat and stir to combine.

4 Pour in the canned products and a little water if necessary. Keep stirring.

5 Allow the mix to cook for 45 minutes over a low heat and check the seasoning before serving.

notes

Once cooked, this can be frozen and reheated when needed.

quick wagyu bresaola  7 days + 24 hr serves 15

1.5 kg wagyu rump
80 g fine salt
15 g white sugar
1 tsp cracked black pepper
1 tsp chopped fresh rosemary
6 crushed juniper berries
½ tsp dry thyme
pinch of cinnamon
pinch of clove

1 Mix all the dry ingredients and keep aside 2 tablespoons of the mixture for step 2. Rub over the beef. Leave to cure for 7 days then rub off the curing mixture and pat dry the meat.

2 Rub the 2 tablespoons of curing mixture over meat, then place in a dehydrator at 50°C for 24-36 hours, depending on the thickness of the beef. The bresaola is ready when it is hard to the touch. Keep chilled and slice when needed. For a quick fuss-free entrée, make a few thin slices and serve as part of an antipasto platter of cured meats with olives. Even slices over grilled prawns or seared scallops would be fantastic.

steak and lager pie

3 hr · serves 4

600 g of beef oyster blade,
   cut into cubes

plain flour

4 onions, cut into rough
   2 x 2-cm dice

8-10 potatoes, peeled and
   cut into 2 x 2-cm dice

50 g butter

extra virgin olive oil

500 ml water, or bouillon mixed
   with beer, or just beer

4 bay leaves

1 tsp dried thyme

salt and ground white pepper

1 Toss the beef cubes with a little flour to coat lightly.

2 Brown the onion, potato and the beef cubes in some oil and butter. Season with salt and white pepper.

3 Add water, beer and/or bouillon, bay leaf and thyme.

4 Transfer the pot to a 160°C oven and cook for 1½-2 hours.

5 The beef will be ready when it breaks easily when pushed with a fork.

6 The stew is now ready to eat or it can be cooled and made into pies using pie/quiche dough or some ready-made puff pastry.

spicy oyster blade salad

1 hr · serves 6

500 g oyster blade steak
75 ml fish sauce
75 ml lime juice
3 small cucumbers, sliced thinly
6 spring onions, sliced thinly
150 g bean sprouts, topped and tailed
1 cup loosely packed fresh mint leaves
200 g cherry tomatoes, halved
½ cup loosely packed coriander leaves
1 stalk lemongrass, thinly sliced
75 ml sweet chilli sauce
1 Tbsp soy sauce

1 Combine the beef with 2 tablespoons of fish sauce and 1 tablespoon of lime juice in a large bowl. Cover and refrigerate for 30 minutes.

2 Drain beef; discard marinade. Cook beef on heated, lightly oiled, grill plate until brown on both sides and to desired doneness. Allow the beef to rest for 5 minutes, then slice thinly.

3 Meanwhile, combine cucumber, spring onion, bean sprouts, mint leaves, tomato and coriander in a bowl.

4 For the dressing, combine remaining fish sauce, lime juice, sliced lemongrass, sweet chilli sauce and soy sauce in a screw-top jar. Shake well.

5 Add beef and dressing to salad, toss gently, arrange and garnish, then serve.

the red salad

20 min   serves 4

600 g red salad leaves such as
   radicchio treviso, red chard,
   red oak leaves, ruby red lettuce,
   red butter lettuce
1 blood plum
1 red onion
4 slow-roasted roma
   tomatoes
2 coal-grilled red capsicums
200 g grilled prime rib steak
4 Tbsp toasted pine nuts
50 g ruby basil

dressing

4 Tbsp sundried tomato pesto
1 tsp chopped garlic
4 Tbsp extra virgin olive oil
1 Tbsp red wine vinegar
salt and ground black pepper

1 Wash all the salad leaves thoroughly and drain on kitchen towel. Arrange the leaves nicely on a large platter to get a very dramatic and colourful effect. Slice the blood plum and red onion into thin circles. Scatter the roasted tomatoes and grilled capsicums over the lettuce.

2 Whisk sundried tomato pesto and garlic with olive oil and red wine vinegar. Season with salt and black pepper.

3 The prime rib steak can be sliced as thinly or thickly as you like. I prefer mine nice and thin so it drapes over the salad rather than crushes it. Drizzle the dressing over the whole salad. Lastly, sprinkle some pine nuts and tear some ruby basil over it.

beef tartare with frozen oysters

30 min

serves 4

2 fresh oysters
240 g beef tenderloin
1–2 Tbsp extra virgin olive oil
200 g watercress
75 g white onion or shallots, diced
30 ml champagne vinegar
100 ml extra virgin olive oil
salt and ground black pepper

1 Open the oysters and freeze with the juice that comes out when you open the oysters.

2 If possible, freeze or chill a plastic cutting board.

3 Cut the beef tenderloin into fine cubes on the chilled cutting board and place into a bowl set over a bowl of ice.

4 Cut the oysters into small cubes or blend until finely chopped in kitchen blender.

5 Mix the frozen oysters with the beef, and using a spatula, fold the mixture together. Season with salt and black pepper, add a little oil to help with shine and smoothness of your mixture. Keep the beef tartare in the fridge until needed – maximum 12 hours, after which the beef will have lost its red colour but still tastes great. Garnish with watercress dressed in champagne vinegar and diced onion or shallot.

the roast...

serves 4

2-3 kg rump roast, netted
2-3 kg ribeye

Heat oven to recommended temperature and weigh meat to estimate cooking time.

1 Place roast on a rack in a roasting pan. Pour a little water into the pan to stop juices burning in pan during cooking.

2 If you have a meat thermometer, insert it into the thickest part of the roast.

3 Cook for estimated time, basting with pan juices throughout cooking. As the water evaporates, add more to the pan.

4 Test to see if the roast is cooked to your liking by squeezing it with tongs: rare feels soft; medium has a little resistance; well done feels quite firm. It's best not to insert a skewer when testing to see if meat is done as it allows the juices, which keep meat tender and tasty, to escape.

5 Alternatively, check the internal temperature of the roast on the meat thermometer. The roast is cooked to:

- rare when the temperature reaches 45-50°C;
- medium when the temperature reaches 60-65°C;
- well-done at 70-75°C.

6 Remove roast from pan and cover loosely with foil. Allow to rest for about 15-20 minutes before carving. This allows the juices to settle. Well-rested meat won't lose any juices onto the plate.

7 For the most tender slices of meat, carve the roast across the grain. Holding the roast with tongs rather than a fork will prevent the juices escaping.

Suggested roasting times per 500 g of meat (For beef roast cuts such as rib, ribeye, tri-tip, tenderloin, and sirloin)			
Oven Temp	Rare	Medium	Well Done
200°C	15-20 minutes	20-25 minutes	25-30 minutes

beef

my wagyu bacon

15 min
+ 7 days

serves 10-15

curing mixture

2 tsp pink salt or nitrate salt
4 Tbsp fine salt
2 Tbsp dark brown sugar

1 Mix everything together and
store in a dry place until needed.

maple cured bacon

1 kg beef brisket or
   wagyu rump
25 g curing mixture
   (*see above*)
maple syrup to coat the meat

1 Rub the meat with curing mixture until well-coated,
then drizzle some maple syrup over the meat and
leave to cure for seven days, well-wrapped and in the
refrigerator.

2 After seven days, the meat would have firmed up
and changed colour to a light brown. This is normal
as the meat oxidises during the curing process.
Remove from wrap and cold smoke the meat (see
smoked bacon recipe this page, for method).

3 Once smoked, place the wagyu in another vacuum
bag and seal. Cook the wagyu at 58°C in a water bath
for 2 hours then cool in ice water.

smoked bacon

1 wok
1 wire rack that fits inside the
   wok or a bamboo steamer
   to place in the steamer
100 g woodchips for smoking

1 Lay the wood chips in the bottom of the wok and
moisten with 2 tablespoons water. Place the cured
meat on the wire rack and cover tightly with aluminum
foil around the wok.

2 Heat wok over a medium fire and once you can
smell the smoke, turn down to low and smoke the
bacon for 30 minutes.

3 Keep the smoked bacon tightly wrapped in the
refrigerator for up to one week or freeze and use when
the craving sets in.

4 Slice thin slices of the bacon and sear in a hot pan.
Serve over a salad of baby spinach and apple. Or
cut into larger pieces and use in the garnish for my
Bourguignon Style Beef Cheeks (*page 74*). This is a
great bacon recipe for those who don't eat pork.

The Stanbroke Story… In my opinion the top producers of Australia's finest quality beef is Stanbroke, one of Australia's most recognised and respected beef cattle producers, with a long history on the land. The family company proudly owns and controls every aspect of its beef business, from breeding to retail-direct delivery. Its operation enables it to achieve complete traceability and quality assurance for customers. For me as a chef, this is very important. And I find that more and more of my guests have a great interest in this too.

My favourite Diamantina beef cuts are:

Tomahawk: A cut of beef rarely found in any butcher shop or restaurant for that matter. It is a joint cut of the ribeye still on the bone, with the bone kept long and the meat from the short rib removed. Every time I serve this I am met with "oohhs and aahhs" and it brings me great pleasure to have cooked and served it on so many different occasions.

Prime rib: A ribeye on the bone means the bone is cut just above the meat. If this cut is roasted, you are sure to have a very dramatic presentation as the bones stick out, and the meat holds on to it. It can also be cut into large impressive steaks, perfect to share at a barbecue.

Oyster blade: Great for braising and an affordable steak. It is a cut from the forequarter and has a rich flavour. The meat is succulent, thanks to the gelatinous tissue in the centre.

Stanbroke's signature beef brand Diamantina is sold around the world in premium retail stores and Stanbroke is one of only a few producers accredited worldwide to export halal certified beef. Working in Malaysia I have found it a challenge to get to know the people that produce the ingredients I use. But with Stanbroke I have built trust and a relationship to last.

Brisket: The belly part of the beef, superb for bacon and corned beef, thanks to its marbling.

Cheek: My favourite cut for braising. You can cook it tender enough to eat with a spoon. Very rich and full of flavour.

Tri-Tip: A very versatile meat that has great flavour and makes a good steak. It lends itself well to braising and curing too.

Tongue: Not to everyone's liking, but try my recipe and you might just change your mind.

tomahawk baked in clay

This dish was first served at dinner with Vega Sicilia – one of Spain's most highly sought-after wines, from winemaker Xavier Ausas. It has since been highly requested by guests who either have eaten it before, or heard about it. Cracking the clay in front of the anticipating guest is always a joy: the smoky fragrance of charcoal-grilled meat, warm spices and moist hay all meld to create a wonderful earthy aroma that suits the meat perfectly.

This dish can be varied to suit your liking. Here is what I like to do:

1 First, source the best possible meat for this. Season it very well; grill it over live coals to get the most aromatic flavour you can give it. Prepare the hay by soaking it in water for 10 minutes and wash it well to remove all dust and short strands of grass. Drain the hay, leave for 10 minutes to drain off as much water as possible. Arrange the hay in a large baking tray and place the beef on top.

2 Neatly cover the beef with more hay and start

rolling your clay. The clay should be about 5-7 mm thick and must cover the whole beef and all the hay.

3 Bake in a 200°C oven for 15 minutes, then take out the tray and leave to rest for 10 minutes. Decorate the tray with a little more hay and crack the clay in front of your friends. Carve the Tomahawk into nice tender slices. You can't go wrong with great beef...

4 Pair with a robust, complex red wine, preferably a Vega Sicilia.

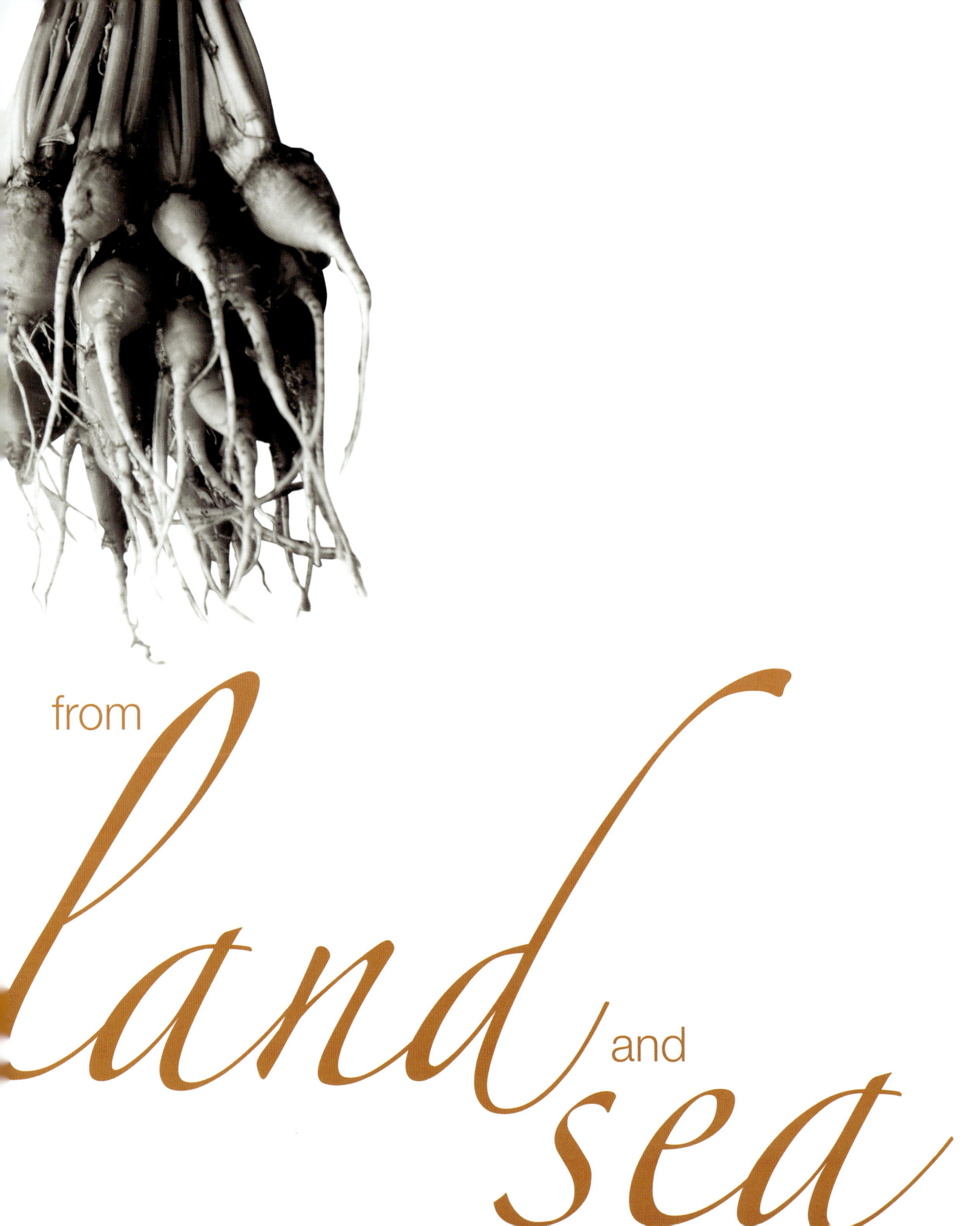

from

land and *sea*

"A lot of farmed fish and seafood we find today is close to wild and of equal quality, but with the benefits of not hurting the wild fish stocks in our seas and of giving nature a chance to recover....."

braised duck with saffron pasta, green peppercorn jus and baby carrots

⏱ 3 hr 🥄 serves 6

braised duck

4-6 large duck legs
1 carrot
1 onion
1 leek
1 stick of celery
5 cloves garlic
1 tsp dried thyme
1 tsp green peppercorns
3 cloves
1 cinnamon stick
2-3 litres chicken stock, or beef stock

1 First, make an incision in the joint of the thigh and the drumstick, but don't cut all the way through, this will help the duck leg to sit flat when you sear it.

2 Cut all the vegetables into 2-cm dice and crush the garlic cloves.

3 Sear the duck legs in a little olive oil until brown and crispy.

4 Remove the legs from the pot and add the vegetables, cook until coloured.

5 Add the thyme, peppercorns, cloves, cinnamon stick and chicken stock.

6 Bring to boil, then put a lid on the pot and place in a 160°C oven for about 2 hours.

7 Once cooked and tender, remove the duck legs, strain the stock and reduce to a sauce. The vegetables will now be very soft but can be kept and eaten with the duck.

baby carrots

200 g organic baby carrot,
    scrubbed and washed
1 tsp cumin seeds
30 g butter
½ tsp sugar
300 ml chicken stock

1 Sauté the baby carrots and cumin seeds in the butter and sugar until they take on a light caramelised colour.

2 Add the chicken stock a little at a time until the carrots are cooked and shiny.

saffron pasta dough

250 g flour
2 whole eggs
5 egg yolks
1 tsp saffron strands
    soaked in 2 tsp hot water

1 Place flour, eggs, yolks and saffron in a bowl and mix with a dough hook until a dough is formed.

2 Knead the dough until smooth, wrap in plastic and rest in the fridge for 30 minutes.

3 Roll the dough to 1-mm thick, 5-cm wide and 25-cm long.

4 Cook the pasta in boiling salted water for about 1 minute.

5 Serve with the braised duck.

To assemble the dish:

Warm up the braised duck and baby carrots, mix well with the pasta and pour a little green peppercorn jus around the dish.

dorper lamb leg baked in clay 1.5 hr  serves 6

1.45 kg dorper easy-carve leg, chilled
1 leek, green part only
2 shallots
2 cloves pink garlic
10 kalamata olives
30 g échiré butter, unsalted
2 Tbsp balsamic vinegar
4 Tbsp olive oil
1 tsp, dried or fresh marjoram
1 tsp chilli flakes
salt and ground black pepper
clay

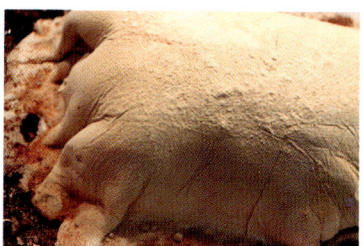

1 Slice leek, shallots and garlic, sauté with olives in Échiré butter, season and cool down. Marinate lamb leg in balsamic vinegar, olive oil, marjoram and chilli flakes. Season with salt and pepper and sear in hot oil.

2 After the lamb leg is seared, stuff it with the leek mixture and place on a large tray. Roll the clay 6-7 mm thick to cover the lamb leg. Bake at 190°C for 45 minutes and rest 10 minutes before carving.

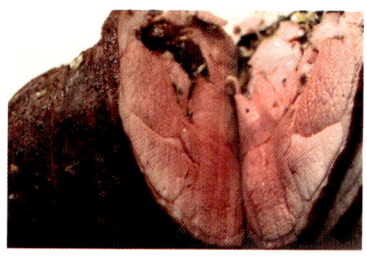

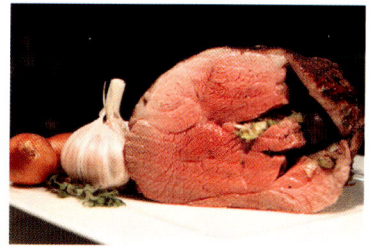

from land and sea

easy-carve dorper lamb leg with fragrant spices

2 hr   serves 6

1 easy-carve dorper lamb leg
500 ml thick coconut milk
250 g desiccated coconut
2 stalks lemongrass,
   slightly crushed
2-3 turmeric leaves
2 kaffir lime leaves
3 Tbsp peanut oil
2 tsp sugar
salt and ground pepper

spice paste:
   40 g galangal, peeled, sliced
   40 g fresh ginger, peeled,
     sliced
   20 g fresh turmeric root,
     peeled, sliced
   4-5 hot red chillies
   2 tsp sea salt

1 Using a mortar and pestle or blender, grind galangal, ginger, turmeric, chillies and sea salt into a paste. In a dry pan, toast the desiccated coconut over low heat, keep stirring until golden brown and fragrant, then add to your spice paste.

2 Heat wok over high heat and fry spice paste for 2-3 minutes in the peanut oil, Add coconut milk, reduce heat and slowly bring to a gentle boil. Stir often then add lemongrass, turmeric leaves, kaffir lime leaves, sugar and season with salt and pepper. Reduce heat to low and simmer for 15 minutes then leave the paste to cool.

3 Once cooled, marinate the lamb leg with this and roast at 160°C for 1 hour until fragrant and when the marinade starts to caramelise.

braised lamb shanks with
cauliflower cocotte

5 hr · serves 6

6 lamb shanks, about 300-400 g each
2 carrots cut into 2-cm slices
2 onions cut into 2-cm slices
2 stalks of leek, cut into 2-cm slices
2 stalks of celery cut into 2-cm slices
6 large ripe tomatoes, cut into quarters
1 head of garlic cut in half horizontally
2 sprigs of fresh rosemary
4 bay leaves
1 Tbsp black peppercorns
500 ml full-bodied red wine,
    a barossa valley shiraz or merlot
extra virgin olive oil
salt and ground pepper
beef stock or water to cover

1 Pre-heat your oven to 160°C.

2 Season the lamb shanks with salt and pepper and sear in a large frying pan with a little olive oil. Turn the shanks over when they are brown and caramelised; this will take a few minutes. Remove the shanks from the pan and add the vegetables, keep cooking until the vegetables are evenly coloured. Add the rosemary, bay leaf and peppercorns, pour in the red wine and reduce by half.

3 Place the lamb shanks in an ovenproof dish and pour the vegetables on top, then top up with beef stock or water to cover. Cover the dish with baking paper then aluminum foil and cook in the oven for 4 hours. The shanks are ready when a knife cuts through them like butter. The lamb shanks will be best eaten after they have cooled in the liquid and reheated the next day. Reduce the cooking liquid to get a nice rich lamb jus. Any extra jus can always be frozen in small containers and used when needed.

cauliflower cocotte

1 large cauliflower
50 g butter
200 ml milk
pinch of cumin seeds
salt

1 Cut off the best florets and keep aside in ice water. Cut the remaining cauliflower into individual florets. Sauté half the florets in butter until they are golden but still with a light crunch. Simmer the remaining florets in the milk with cumin seeds and salt. Once soft, take out the florets and blend to a smooth purée.

2 Layer small cocotte moulds with sautéed cauliflower and a layer of cauliflower purée on top. Garnish with the raw cauliflower.

from land and sea

venison rissole

1 hr   serves 6

50 g bread crumbs

100 ml milk

350 g minced venison leg

15 g chopped truffles

5 g truffle oil

100 g sautéed button
    mushroom

5 g chopped fresh thyme

15 g chopped fresh parsley

1 whole egg

25 g st agur blue cheese,
    or other mild blue cheese

15 g venison or beef jus

salt and ground pepper

knob of butter for cooking

1 Soak bread crumbs in milk while preparing the meat. Place all other ingredients in a mixing bowl and mix with the paddle to a well-mixed farci. This can be done by hand if you don't mind getting your hands in there. Add the soaked bread crumbs to lighten the mix and mix well. Roll into round balls about 45 g each, keep refrigerated until needed.

To cook the rissoles:

Heat a little olive oil and a knob of butter in a frying pan and cook until the meat is nice and brown all around then, transfer to a warm oven to cook through.

quail with warm caponata salad

warm caponata salad

14 hr prep + 30 min   serves 6

1 medium-sized aubergine

1 medium-sized onion

2 sticks of celery

1 clove garlic

1 roma tomato

sea salt and ground black pepper

sugar

2 Tbsp extra virgin olive oil

sourdough croutons made from day-old sourdough bread

1 tsp capers

20 kalamata olives, pitted and dried for 30 minutes in a hot oven

1 Tbsp roasted pine nuts

1 Tbsp chopped fresh basil

15 leaves rocket lettuce

1 Dice all the vegetables to 1.5 cm cubes. Sauté each vegetable separately. Peel and deseed the Roma tomato, cut in quarters and sprinkle with salt, sugar and black pepper, leave for 12-24 hours.

2 When ready to serve the salad, sauté all ingredients in olive oil, check seasoning and serve with grilled honey and orange marinated quail.

grilled honey and orange marinated quail

2 hr prep + 30 min   serves 6

4 whole quails

marinade:

1 Tbsp wholegrain mustard

1 Tbsp tasmanian leatherwood honey

juice and zest of 1 orange

1 Tbsp olive oil

sea salt

coarsely ground black pepper

1 Whisk together the ingredients for the marinade.

2 Debone the quails and marinate for at least 1 hour but preferably longer.

3 Heat the grill in your oven and place the quails in an ovenproof dish under the grill and cook until caramelised. Serve with warm caponata salad and a glass of Rosé.

lamb shank pithivier

45 min   serves 4

2 cooked lamb shanks

4 Tbsp lamb jus from braising the lamb shanks

200 g tuscan black cabbage, or savoy cabbage

200 g cooked du puy lentils

800 g puff pastry, rolled 3-4 mm thick

sea salt and ground white pepper

1 whole egg for egg wash

1 Remove the meat from the bones and separate it with your fingers. Melt the jus and mix with the meat, season with salt and pepper.

2 Cook the cabbage quickly in salted water and cool in ice water to keep the bright green colour. Cut the puff pastry into eight 12-cm circles. Brush four pastry circles with egg and, using a small sharp knife, make a cut from the centre of the circle towards the outside. Place 2 tablespoons lentils, followed by cabbage and lamb shank meat in the centre of

each of the four remaining circles. Transfer all the pastries to the fridge and leave to firm up for about 10 minutes.

3 Once the pastries are firm and easy to handle, lay one cut pastry circle over the lamb shank filling and press the two circles gently on the sides so they stick together. Use a large ring cutter to cut away the surrounding pastry and keep the pies chilled until ready to bake. Bake in a 190°C hot oven for 14 minutes until golden brown. Enjoy with a nice green salad dressed with French dressing.

melting dorper lamb shoulder

3 hr   serves 6

2 kg lamb shoulder

2 medium-sized onions

10 spring onions

2 large thumb-size pieces of ginger

3 star anise

1 tsp fennel seeds

1 tsp white peppercorns

3 large dried chillies

2 chinese cardamon pods

2 cinnamon sticks

1 Tbsp salted dried tangerine peel, or the zest from half a fresh mandarin

100 g chinese rock sugar

3 Tbsp dark soya sauce

5 Tbsp light soya sauce

250 ml yellow chinese cooking wine

75 ml peanut oil

1 Trim the lamb of any fats and sinew. Bring a large pot of water to boil and blanch the lamb in this for 2 minutes. Cool in ice water then pat dry. Slice the onion, spring onion and ginger. Mix all the dry spices and rock sugar with the sliced onions and ginger. Pound in a mortar and pestle until well broken down and aromatic. Rub this mixture over the lamb, then pour the sauces and wine over and coat the meat by basting it with sauce and spice mixture. Leave to marinate for one hour.

2 Heat the peanut oil in a large pot and sear the lamb on all sides. Pour in half of the marinade and reduce until sticky. Roll the lamb in the sticky reduction, then pour in the remaining marinade. Bring to boil, then cover with a lid and braise in a 160°C warm oven for 2 hours. Check half-way through the cooking time that there is still some marinade left in the pot – if you feel it looks a bit dry and risks burning, add 250 ml of water and continue cooking. Once cooked, remove from the oven and serve with steamed rice and sautéed Asian greens.

from land and sea

roast chicken in lotus leaf

1.5 hr   serves 6

1 large free range organic
    chicken 1.6-2 kg

50 ml cognac

1 bunch fresh thyme

10 g butter

1 lemon

1 head garlic

2 bay leaves

sea salt and ground white
pepper

1 large dried lotus leaf,
    available at chinese grocers

olive oil

1 Wash the chicken and dry thoroughly with paper towel. Using your fingers, separate the skin from the breast meat, down to the legs. Season the chicken with sea salt and white pepper under and on the skin. Pour the cognac into the cavity and under the skin. Roughly chop the thyme and mix with the butter. Peel the zest of the lemon and crush the whole head of garlic, fill the cavity with this and the bay leaves. Rub the butter mixture under the skin of the chicken, in the cavity and on the outside of the chicken. Tie the legs together to hold the filling in the cavity.

2 Soak the lotus leaf for a few minutes in warm water. Rub the inside of the leaf with a little olive oil then wrap the chicken in the leaf. Roast at 160°C for 45 minutes, then turn the oven up to 190°C and cook for another 10–15 minutes, if you want more colour on the skin of the chicken. Remove the chicken from the oven and leave to rest for 15 minutes. Open the leaf and enjoy the aroma. Carve the chicken and serve with your favourite salad and roast vegetables.

market fish baked in paper

45 min   serves 4

4 fish fillets: john dory, garoupa,
    sea bass
4 stalks of lemongrass
1 x 4-cm piece of ginger
4 red chilli
4 spring onions
4 Tbsp light soya sauce
1 tsp sesame oil
4 Tbsp peanut oil
pak choy, choy sum or kai lan
few sprigs or coriander
parchment/baking paper

1 Crush lemongrass in a mortar. With a sturdy knife, slice the ginger, chilli and spring onions thinly.

2 Mix soya sauce and sesame oil with the vegetables, heat the peanut oil until very hot and pour into the soya mix to release their aroma. Marinate the fish fillets in this for 1–2 hours.

3 Trim, wash and blanch the Asian vegetables. Cool in ice water.

4 Place a large sheet of baking paper on a baking tray. Put some of the soya mix in the centre of the paper and arrange some Asian greens over it. Place the fish on top of the greens and complete with the sliced vegetables from the marinade and a few coriander sprigs.

5 Bring the edges of the baking paper together and fold to seal the parcel. Bake at 180°C for 8–10 minutes.

6 Be careful when opening the parcel since it will be steaming hot.

abalone risotto

45 min serves 4

600 ml chicken stock

2 medium-sized onions

6 button mushrooms

1 portobello mushroom

20-30 shimeji mushrooms

handful fresh wild mushrooms
such as chanterelle, cep,
blue foot

4 dried boletus mushrooms
or dried porcini soaked
in warm water

olive oil

50 g butter

150 g carnaroli risotto rice

6 cooked jade tiger abalones

1 Bring the chicken stock to boil and keep aside.

2 Chop the onions finely, slice the button and Portobello mushrooms. Separate the shimeji mushrooms and wash the wild mushrooms. Heat a little olive oil in a large pot and add the chopped onions. Cook the onions until caramelised and evenly browned. Add the mushrooms and butter. Cook until the mushrooms are softened and shiny.

3 Add the Carnaroli rice and stir to toast the rice for a few minutes. This will ensure you get a great end result with the most flavour possible. Start by adding half of the chicken stock and after it has been absorbed, add the remaining stock a little at a time, stirring all the while. Once the rice is cooked, let it rest for a few minutes, covered, on the side of the stove.

4 Heat a little oil in a frying pan and colour the cooked abalone. Once warm and nicely browned, slice the abalone and arrange on top of the risotto. Garnish with rocket flowers or some fine cress.

loch fyne scottish salmon, vanilla poached salsify, juniper cream sauce

45 min · serves 4

vanilla poached salsify

500 g fresh salsify
1 litre milk
1 vanilla bean, split and scraped
1 tsp fresh thyme leaves
2 bay leaves
2 crushed cloves of garlic

1 Peel the salsify and place in an ovenproof dish with all the ingredients and cook at 160°C for 30 minutes.

Tip: Salsify is a European root vegetable with a dark brown skin that needs to be peeled off before cooking. It has a sweet clean earthy flavour. If you can't find fresh salsify, you can use celeriac or even parsnip.

juniper sauce

200 g cream
100 ml milk
50 ml white wine
10 crushed juniper berries
2 x 1-cm strips of lemon zest
sea salt and ground white pepper

1 Bring everything to boil and simmer until the sauce has the viscosity of pouring cream. Strain and season with sea salt and white pepper.

4 x 130 g salmon fillets
1 fennel bulb
100 g french black radish
dill tops for garnish
extra virgin olive oil
sea salt and ground white pepper

When serving:

- Season the salmon fillets and sear the skin side in hot oil. Transfer to a hot oven to cook for another 2-3 minutes. Slice the fennel 1-cm thick and cook with the poached salsify in the same pan. Deglaze with a little white wine, then arrange on warm plates. Slice the black radish thinly and arrange on the plate with the fennel and salsify.

- Lean the salmon on the vegetables, garnish with sprigs of dill.

- Pour the sauce around the fish, a little caviar or fish roe can be added to the sauce for extra indulgence...

seafood cassoulet with grilled yellowtail kingfish and marinated bresaola

24 hr soaking +
1 hr cooking time

serves 4

4 x 130 g yellowtail kingfish
  fillets, grilled

500 g dried cannellini beans
2 whole roma tomatoes
2 celery sticks
2 leek, white part only
2 medium-sized onions
4 litres chicken stock
4 bay leaves
small bunch fresh thyme
8 parsley stalks

1 Soak the beans overnight in cold water in the fridge. Peel and cut all the vegetables into large pieces and keep aside until needed. Rinse and strain the beans the following day and simmer with the rest of the ingredients until the beans are very soft. The stock should be reduced enough so that a minimal amount of stock will be strained out. Once cooked and cooled down, remove all the herbs and vegetables.

marinated bresaola

1 red chilli
1 whole shallot
1 clove garlic
1 lime
40 g grated parmesan cheese
100 ml extra virgin olive oil
freshly ground black pepper
200 g bresaola, air-dried beef

1 Chop the chili, shallot and garlic finely and place in a bowl. Grate the zest of the lime and add together with the Parmesan. Top up with olive oil and season with black pepper. Slice the bresaola very thinly and leave to marinate for a minimum of 6 hours. Serve this marinated bresaola with grilled kingfish and seafood cassoulet or on its own with tasty sourdough bread.

When serving

- Heat up the cassoulet and add some semi-dried cherry tomato, baby romain lettuce, smoked fish, cut prawn meat, fresh mussel, squid and freshly chopped thyme.

- Serve with a grilled Yellowtail Kingfish and marinated bresaola.

steamed turbot with warm scallop terrine

1.5 hr   serves 4

4 x 130 g fillets of turbot

1 litre milk
2 shallots
1 leek, white part only
1 lemon
1 Tbsp freshly chopped dill
1 Tbsp freshly chopped thyme
1 Tbsp sea salt
1 tsp white peppercorns

for scallop mousseline

200 g scallop meat
50 g cream
half an egg
salt and ground white pepper
1 leek, green part only
1 Tbsp chopped chives

mustard cream

100 g whipping cream
1 Tbsp wholegrain mustard

200 g fresh spinach or
    other green leafy vegetable,
    steamed
sea asparagus and snow pea
    shoots for garnish

1 Pour the milk into a large saucepot. Slice the shallots and the white part of the leek into thin rings. Peel the zest of the lemon and add together with dill, thyme, salt and peppercorns to the pot of milk. Bring to boil and simmer for 5 minutes. Keep a watchful eye on it because the milk may boil over when you are not looking. Transfer this flavourful milk to an ovenproof dish and place in a steamer.

2 For the scallop mousseline, place the scallop, cream and egg in a blender or a Pacojet container. Blend until smooth, Blend until smooth, then add chopped chives, season with salt and white pepper. Blanch the green part of the leek in boiling salted water until tender. Remove from the water and cool in ice water. Layer a small terrine or cake mould with blanched leek leaves and start layering with scallop mousseline. The terrine should have leek on the top and bottom layer.

3 For mustard cream, whip the whipping cream to soft peaks, add the mustard and whisk until it is firm and can be spooned nicely without running off the spoon.

4 Place the scallop terrine in the steamer. Place the turbot fillets in the warm milk in the steamer and steam for 8-10 minutes.

When serving:

■ Remove the terrine and slice into 8 triangles and arrange on warm plates. Take out the turbot and strain the milk. Using a hand blender, blitz the milk until foamy.

■ Place steamed vegetables on the plates with scallop terrine on the side. Arrange the turbot on the vegetables; peel back the skin of the fish in order to show its shiny flesh.

■ Spoon the milk foam around the fish and place a nice teaspoon of mustard cream on the turbot.

■ Garnish with naturally salty sea asparagus and snow pea shoots.

white fish with summer vegetables

45 min   serves 4

4 x 130 g fillets of white fish
    such as: cod, sea bass,
    halibut, barramundi

1 yellow capsicum
8 small new season potatoes
6 small courgettes or
    1 medium zucchini
4 Tbsp toasted pine nuts
2 cloves garlic
150 g baby spinach
extra virgin olive oil
25 g fresh basil
50 ml sunflower oil
sea salt and ground black
    pepper

1 Roast the yellow capsicum in hot oven until the skin blisters and turns black. Place the capsicum in a bowl and cover with cling wrap and leave to steam for 10 minutes. When cool enough to handle, peel the capsicum and cut into long strips 1-cm wide.

2 Slice the potatoes about 3-mm thick and sauté in a little oil until soft and tender, but still holding together. Slice the courgettes lengthwise and add to the potatoes. Sauté until tender then add capsicum and pine nuts.

Season and keep warm. Season and sear the fish fillets of your choice. If they are nice thick fillets, place them in an oven heated to 160°C to cook through, rather than turning them in a frying pan.

3 Slice the garlic and sauté with baby spinach for a few seconds, so that spinach just wilts and still keeps its bright colour. Place basil and sunflower oil in a blender and blend until a smooth green oil is formed. Strain the oil and keep refrigerated until needed.

When serving:

■ Arrange the vegetables on warm plates with a fillet of fish on top. Add a spoonful of sautéed spinach on each fish and drizzle a little basil oil around the plate.

braised jade tiger abalone with steamed duck and soba noodles 🕐 4 hr 🥄 serves 4

braised jade tiger abalone

4 live jade tiger abalones
100 ml dry sake
250 ml chicken consommé
1 sheet kombu seaweed
sea salt

1 Place the live abalones, still in their shells, into a baking dish and cover with sake, stock and the sheet of kombu.

2 Cover tightly with cling film and steam for 3-4 hours until the abalones are tender.

soba noodles

400 g fresh soba noodles

1 Bring a pot of salted water to the boil and boil the fresh soba noodles for 3-4 minutes. Taste one to see that it is tender but still has a bite to it. Once cooked, strain and cool in ice water.

2 Drain the soba noodles and keep in the refrigerator until needed.

steamed duck

1 small duck or duckling
75 ml dark soya sauce
25 ml light soya sauce
2 Tbsp honey
1 thumb-size piece of ginger
    sliced finely
6 spring onions
1 chinese cardamom, crushed
1 dried red chilli
ground white pepper

1 Rub the duck all over and inside with soya sauces and honey. Fill the cavity with the ginger slices, spring onions, Chinese cardamom and red chilli. Season with white pepper and leave overnight if time allows. If you are hungry, steam it at the same time as the abalone.

When serving:

■ Remove the duck from the steamer and cut into portions. Slice the abalone and serve with abalone sauce thickened with a little wheat starch and cooked soba noodles.

salt-baked jade tiger abalone

🕐 30 min   🥄 serves 4

4 x 130 g live jade tiger
    abalones

40 g soaked wakame seaweed

100 ml japanese sake

1 Tbsp sea urchin paste

500 g rock salt

1 egg white

sea salt

1 Scoop the live abalone out of its shell, using a spoon. Leave the liver on the body but cut away the mouth of the abalone using a sharp knife. Place a small mound of wakame in the bottom of each shell and splash some sake over it. Smear the flat side of the abalone with sea urchin paste. Place the abalone on top of the wakame, sea urchin side facing up. Top with another mound of wakame and drizzle more sake over it.

2 Mix the rock salt with the egg white and a little water. Place a 1-cm layer of rock salt in a baking dish and place the abalone on top, shell side down. Completely cover the abalone with the remaining rock salt. It should be about 2-cm thick on top.

3 Heat the baking dish for 1 minute over a medium heat then cook under a hot grill for another 1-2 minutes. Once done, crack the salt open and unveil the abalone.

4 Slice and eat as is, and enjoy its clean oceanic flavour.

grilled prawns with eggplant, chorizo and wagyu bresaola

 45 min serves 4

12 large prawns, preferably
   spencer gulf prawns

1 large eggplant

1 red capsicum

1 yellow capsicum

3 red chillies

3 cloves garlic

1 chorizo sausage

4 semi-dried tomatoes

100 ml extra virgin olive oil

50 g wagyu bresaola *(recipe on
   page 78)*

sea salt and ground black
   pepper

1 Peel and devein the prawns, leave the heads on but use scissors and cut the prawns just behind their eyes to remove the sharp shell that is in the centre.

2 Cut all the vegetables into small cubes. Finely chop the chilli and garlic. Slice the chorizo into thin round slices. Heat the olive oil over low heat and cook the chorizo until the oil turns red and fragrant. Add all the vegetables and cook until soft and the chorizo oil is absorbed. Season with salt and black pepper. It is supposed to be a nice balance of chorizo, chilli and garlic flavour. Season the prawns and grill in a hot pan or on a barbecue for a great smoky flavour.

3 Arrange the chorizo and vegetables on 4 plates. Lean the prawns on the vegetables and scatter thin slices of wagyu bresaola around the dish.

I always try to use Spencer Gulf prawns from South Australia for their excellent flavour and as they are caught sustainably.

snacks

"
Bring variety to your dinner parties. Included in this book are my little secrets from the professional kitchen. A lot of our guests are very curious and want to know our secrets. "

foie gras praline

30 min   serves 6

100 g raw foie gras

salt and ground pepper

30 g cocoa butter

25 g feuillantine

30 g green pistachio nuts, chopped

1 Season foie gras with salt and pepper then coat them in cocoa butter, sear and cool down in the fridge. Melt the remaining cocoa butter and pour over the feuillantine, stir to coat and leave to set in the refrigerator. Shape the foie gras into small rounds and place a little feuillantine in the centre. Roll in chopped green pistachio nuts. Serve chilled.

foie gras tuile

20 min — serves 6

50 g foie gras fat
25 g maltodextrin de-19 sugar
50 g flour
50 g egg white
sea salt flakes

1 Melt the foie gras fat and stir with maltodextrin and flour. Add the egg white last and stir to a smooth batter. Spread the batter thinly on a silpat mat and brush with more melted foie gras fat and sprinkle with sea salt.

2 Bake at 190℃ for 3-4 minutes. Allow to cool, then break into large pieces.

3 Store and serve at room temperature.

smoked salmon pillow

1.5 hr — makes 50 pillows

300 g lamourette/baguette bread dough
100 g sour cream
2 Tbsp chopped dill
2 Tbsp chopped chives
100 g smoked salmon
2 Tbsp ocean trout roe
50 pieces borage / cucumber cress

1 Roll the lamourette dough very thinly in a pasta machine. Place the dough on a floured surface and fold it over like you would if making ravioli, pressing down to make sure the dough sticks. Cut with a crinkle cutter into square shapes, 3 x 3-cm.

2 Leave dough to proof in a warm place until double in size and bake at 190℃ for 4-5 minutes. The dough should puff up and form a hollow pillow.

3 Mix sour cream with chopped herbs and smoked salmon. Make a small hole in the pillow and pipe in the sour cream filling, garnish with trout roe and borage cress.

beetroot macarons

1 + 6 hr

makes 50 macarons

500 ml beetroot juice
180 g sugar
10 g metil (*see glossary section under* texturas products)
30 g egg white powder

1 Combine beetroot juice and sugar and boil. Measure out 420 ml beetroot syrup and bring to simmer. Using a handheld blender, blitz in the metil and egg white powder, transfer to a mixing bowl fitted with a whisk and whip until tripled in size.

2 Pipe little macarons using a plain nozzle and dry at 65°C until dry and crispy, about 4-6 hours.

horseradish filling for beetroot macarons

100 g grated horseradish
100 g crème fraiche
25 g chopped chives
salt and ground white pepper

1 Mix all ingredients well and season with salt and white pepper.

saffron and metil macarons

 1+6 hr

 makes
50 macarons

- 500 ml water
- 1 g saffron
- 180 g sugar
- 10 g metil (*see glossary under textturas products*)
- 30 g egg white powder

1 Boil water and saffron together. Measure out 420 ml saffron syrup and bring syrup to simmer. Using a handheld blender, blitz in the metil and egg white powder.

2 Transfer to a mixing bowl fitted with a whisk and whip until tripled in size.

3 Pipe little macarons using a plain nozzle and dry at 65°C for 4-6 hours until dry and crispy.

parmesan agar spaghetti

24 hr + 45 min

serves 6

1 kg grated parmesan cheese
1 litre water
agar-agar powder, 2.5 g per 100 ml liquid

1 Bring the Parmesan and water to boil. Once boiling, pour into a tall clear container.

2 Place cling film on the surface of the liquid.

3 The liquid will settle into 3 layers: The top is a fat with strong Parmesan flavour; the middle is the Parmesan water you will use for the spaghetti; the bottom is a Parmesan jelly that is quite hard and can be used in other recipes.

4 Once set overnight, remove the top layer and put aside. Take out the Parmesan water and measure 2.5 g agar-agar for every 100 ml Parmesan water. Bring Parmesan water to boil and dissolve agar-agar into this.

5 Use a syringe to fill thin plastic tubes/hose with this; chill in ice water for 2 minutes then put the syringe back in the tube/hose and blow out the spaghetti.

6 Coat the spaghetti with a little Parmesan fat and serve in Chinese spoons with a piece of gold leaf for added luxury.

black potato pebbles

45 min   makes 25 black pebble potatoes

25 chat potatoes, boiled

80 g kalamata olives, pits removed
120 g squid ink
2 g egg white
1 tsp olive oil

1 Roast the olives in a 160℃ oven until shrivelled but still purple in colour.

2 Transfer the olives to a food processor and add squid ink, egg white and olive oil. Blend this mixture until perfectly smooth and keep refrigerated.

3 Roll a boiled cocktail potato in the mixture and make sure the potato is well coated. Bake in a hot oven for 5 minutes for the mixture to set on the potato.

polenta-based croquettes

45 min   makes 25 croquettes

500 ml milk
100 g polenta
50 ml extra virgin olive oil
50 g butter
25 g parmesan cheese
100 g smoked cod
3 tbsp chopped dill
grated zest from 1 lemon
sea salt and ground white pepper
1 egg
50 g panko breadcrumbs

1 Bring the milk to boil, and pour in the polenta in a thin stream. Whisk to avoid any lumps forming.

2 Cook for 7-8 minutes and then add the olive oil and butter. Keep whisking all the time and once the polenta is cooked, add the Parmesan cheese, smoked cod, dill and lemon zest. Season with salt and white pepper.

3 Pour into a buttered tray and leave to cool and set in the fridge.

4 Cut into desired shape. Dip croquettes in egg, then panko, deep fry at 160°C until golden and crispy.

oyster pearls

1 hr   serves 15-20

4 oysters
250 ml still mineral water
1 tsp squid ink
2 g algin (*see glossary section under* texturas products)
1½ tsp calcic (*see glossary section under* texturas products)
500 ml water

1 Blend oysters with ice-cold still mineral water, then add the squid ink and strain.

2 Blend in the algin and vacuum out the air bubbles.

3 Dissolve the calcic in 500 ml water and drip the pearls into this.

You will find these croquette recipes great for a big party. You can make a large batch easily. The polenta croquettes can be cut into any shape, whereas the potato version will not allow that. Croquettes can easily be varied by changing the flavourings. Use prawns and chilli flakes for a spicy croquette, or ham and Gruyère cheese for that familiar Croque Monsieur flavour.

potato-based croquettes

45 min

makes
25 croquettes

4 waxy potatoes, desiree
  or pink skin variety
2 Tbsp plain flour
100 g smoked cod
3 Tbsp chopped dill
grated zest from 1 lemon
sea salt and ground white
  pepper
1 egg
50 g panko bread crumbs

1 Boil the potatoes in salted water. Once soft, mash into a smooth purée. Mix in flour, smoked cod, dill and lemon zest. Season with sea salt and white pepper.

2 Roll the mixture into little balls or short logs. Place in the refrigerator and keep cold until needed. This will help the croquettes to firm up and hold their shape. Once ready to cook, roll the croquettes in egg, then panko.

3 Deep fry at 160°C until golden and crispy. Keep warm in an oven until needed. That is, if you can resist them...

desserts

"Coffee is everywhere in Italy but go to the place that has no tables and chairs... the espresso is so smooth, it will leave you begging for more..."

one-minute chocolate tart

1.5 hr   serves 10-12

coffee sable crust

100 g icing sugar
25 g sugar
200 g butter
1 whole egg
250 g flour
15 g coffee extract

1 Place sugars and butter in a kitchen blender and use the paddle attachment to mix until white and creamy. Add the egg, then on a slow speed, mix in the flour and coffee extract. Allow the dough to rest in the refrigerator for 1 hour before using. Roll the dough on a cold floured surface to about 2–3 mm thin and set in small tart rings about 8–10 cm in diameter and 1–1.5 cm tall. Freeze the dough in the tart rings. When frozen, transfer to a baking tray and blind bake at 190°C for 3–4 minutes to cook the dough.

This is the tart crust for my One-Minute Chocolate Tart, but it can be filled with a filling of your choice.

chocolate tart filling

 5 min  serves 10-12

1 whole egg
2 egg yolks
2 ½ Tbsp sugar
100 g ganache
  (*recipe follows*)
1 Tbsp flour

1 Whisk eggs and sugar together, fold in the ganache and flour. Pour into a siphon and charge with 2 gas cartridges. Shake the bottle thoroughly and extract into the blind-baked tart shell, about 1–1.5 cm high.

2 Bake at 190°C for only 1 minute.

chocolate ganache

 15 min + 1 min baking time  serves 10-12

70 g chocolate
80 g cream

1 Chop the chocolate into small pieces and place in a bowl. Bring the cream to boil and pour over the chocolate, stir with a spatula to create a smooth chocolate ganache.

chocolate soil

 30 min  serves 10-12

200 g sugar
250 g ground almond
110 g valrhona
  cocoa powder
150 g cake flour
1 tsp salt
125 g melted butter

1 Simply mix everything together until it resembles crumbly soil. Bake at 150°C for 20 minutes

To assemble the dish:

Once the tart is out of the oven, dust it with cocoa powder. Remove the tart ring carefully and garnish the plate with a brush stroke of ganache. Place a spoonful of chocolate soil over the ganache and top with a scoop of your favourite ice cream. It takes only one minute to assemble this tart, hence the name.

chocolate fondant

45 min   serves 10

175 g araguani, valrhona
   chocolate 72 percent
140 g butter
3 egg yolks
4 whole eggs
3 Tbsp flour
125 g sugar

1 Melt the chocolate and butter over warm water. Whisk the eggs, flour and sugar together, then fold the egg mixture into the chocolate mixture. Butter some aluminium cups and pour the chocolate filling into the cups.

2 Let the puddings set in the fridge overnight for the best result. If you can't wait, then bake the puddings straightaway for 8-9 minutes at 190°C. Allow the puddings to rest in the aluminium cup for 1 minute before you turn it upside down to unmould the pudding.

3 Serve with fresh berries, chocolate sauce and blackcurrant and vodka sorbet (*see page 157*).

my chocolate soufflé

30 min   serves 6-8

chocolate soufflé base

- **75 g valrhona guanaja chocolate**
- **8 egg yolks**
- **120 g sugar**
- **400 ml milk**
- **80 g wheat starch**
- **20 g valrhona cocoa powder**

1 Melt the chocolate and keep aside. Whisk egg yolk and sugar until pale and creamy. Mix cold milk, wheat starch and cocoa powder in a pot and heat over medium heat. Whisk this mixture until it thickens. It will become very thick. Pour the egg mix into the thickened milk and whisk to combine. Add the chocolate to the mix and using a spatula, scrape the sides and bottom of the pot to catch any starch that might be sticking to the pot.

just before serving

- **100 g chocolate soufflé base**
- **60 g egg white**
- **30 g sugar**

1 Melt the chocolate base if it's a little thick. Whisk the egg white to soft peaks and slowly add the sugar. Do not over-beat the egg white. You want it to stay creamy and at soft peak stage. Fold the egg white into the soufflé base in 3 batches. Bake at 190°C for 7-9 minutes depending on your oven.

my lemon soufflé

1 hr   serves 6-8

lemon soufflé base

200 ml milk
40 g wheat starch
3 lemons for zest and juice
50 ml limoncello
4 egg yolks
80 g sugar

1 Whisk together cold milk and starch. Bring to boil and cook over a low heat for 5 minutes until the mixture is very thick. Add the zest of 3 lemons and the juice of 2 together with the Limoncello. Whisk until very smooth and cover with cling film to keep the heat.

2 Whisk egg yolks and sugar till light and fluffy, then whisk into the lemon mixture.

just before serving

100 g lemon soufflé base
60 g egg white
30 g sugar

1 Whisk the egg white to soft peaks and slowly add the sugar. Do not over-beat the egg white. You want it to stay creamy and at soft peak stage. Fold the egg white into the soufflé base in 3 batches. Bake at 190°C for 7–9 minutes depending on your oven.

desserts

almond and milk panna cotta

1 + 4 hr   serves 12

250 g almond kernels
250 g cream
150 g sugar
1 vanilla bean, split and
    scraped
8 gelatine leaves
750 ml water,
    still mineral water
500 g whipped cream

1 Soak kernels in water overnight. Heat the cream, sugar and vanilla, melt the gelatine in the cream. Add the almonds and mineral water. Blend until smooth, then strain. Leave to cool and thicken in the refrigerator. When it's almost set, fold in the whipped cream.

2 Pour into moulds and set in the refrigerator. Once set, it can be frozen.

brioche pain perdu

30 min   serves 6

brioche loaf cut into
    6 x 2 x 2-cm batonets
30 g sugar
250 ml milk
180 g egg
30 g butterscotch schnapps
    or frangelico
1 vanilla bean, split and
    scraped
clarified butter
icing sugar for dusting

1 Blend everything except brioche and the vanilla bean.

2 Strain the mix into a bowl, add the vanilla bean seeds into the mix.

3 Dip the brioche in the mixture and pan fry with clarified butter until coloured.

4 Dust with icing sugar and cook until a caramel is formed

5 Stir the brioche in the caramel to form a nice crust.

6 Serve warm with Prune and Armagnac parfait (*see page 161*) or Green Apple jelly (*see below*).

green apple jelly

3 gelatine leaves
300 g green apple purée
    or juice

1 Soak the gelatine in 100 g apple purée for 10 minutes. Heat this purée to about 60-80°C to melt the gelatine, then add the remaining purée. Stir well and pour into a tray. Set in the fridge. Spoon the jelly from the tray, and serve with the brioche pain perdu.

coconut curd

30 min **serves 8**

300 g coconut purée
30 g icing sugar
6 g agar-agar
15 g malibu rum

1 Boil purée with sugar and whisk in the agar agar. Simmer the mix for 3-4 minutes.

2 Add the Malibu rum once the pot is off the stove. Pour into a container and let it set.

3 Once cold and set, transfer to a blender and blend until smooth. Use for macaron fillings and as fillings between two tuiles. I would also smear this on a plate and serve with caramelised bananas or pineapple.

orange and vanilla curd

30 min **serves 8**

135 ml orange juice
2 g agar-agar powder
135 g sugar
1 vanilla bean, split and scraped
135 g whole eggs, about 2 large eggs
50 ml grand marnier
170 g unsalted butter

1 Bring orange juice, agar-agar, sugar, scraped vanilla bean and whole eggs to boil. Keep whisking this mixture as it heats up and during its cooking. Boil the mixture for 2 minutes then transfer to a kitchen blender and blend on medium speed. Slowly add the Grand Marnier and butter little by little. Blend until perfectly smooth, then transfer to a non-metallic container and chill. Store in the refrigerator until needed for macarons (*see page 168*). This curd can also be used to fill a tart shell then covered with a little meringue for an orange version of the classic lemon curd tart.

crème caramel, blackberry sponge, muscat espuma

1.5 hr   serves 12

crème caramel

300 g sugar for caramel
1 vanilla bean, split and scraped
1 litre milk
10 eggs
2 egg yolks
140 g sugar

1 Start by placing the 300 g sugar in a heavy-bottomed saucepot over a medium high heat to melt the sugar. Once the sugar starts to melt, you can swirl the pot around to melt the sugar evenly but do not stir the sugar. Stirring it will make it crystallise and turn hard as a rock. When the sugar turns a golden brown, you only have about 2 minutes before it burns. You want your caramel to have a nice brown cognac colour. Pour the caramel into your crème caramel ramekins and leave to set.

2 Add the vanilla to the milk. Heat until it just starts to boil and remove from the heat. Lightly whisk the eggs, egg yolks and sugar in a bowl. Don't overdo this stage because otherwise your mixture will be full of bubbles and you won't get the smooth texture you are looking for. While whisking, pour the warm milk into the egg mixture and whisk to avoid cooking the eggs. Strain the mixture, then pour into the crème caramel ramekins. Bake in a water bath for 45-50 minutes at 110°C or until just set in the middle. Once cooked, remove the tray and leave to cool at room temperature for 20 minutes. After that, the crème caramel can be placed in the refrigerator and eaten when cold.

3 When serving, run a thin knife around the edge of the ramekin and turn it upside down onto a plate. The caramel will melt and the crème caramel will slide out and onto your plate. Serve with a broken-up blackberry yoghurt sponge cake and Muscat espuma.

blackberry yoghurt sponge cake

3 whole eggs
125 g sugar
12 g baking powder
200 g flour
125 g yoghurt
125 g melted butter
40 g blackberries
75 g blackberry purée

1 Whisk eggs and sugar until white and fluffy. Sift baking powder and flour together and fold into the eggs. Add the yoghurt and then the melted butter. Spray a 2-cm high cake tin with baking spray. Pour the batter into cake tin. Sprinkle the blackberries on top and bake at 170°C for 10 minutes.

2 Once the cake is cooked, remove from the oven and pour the blackberry purée over the top and leave to soak into the cake. Leave to set and keep refrigerated. Break into irregular pieces and serve with crème caramel and Muscat espuma.

muscat espuma

400 ml milk

100 g cream

100 ml chambers muscat,
   sweet dessert wine

50 g sugar

4 g xantana
   (*see glossary section
   under* texturas products)

1 Heat the milk, cream, sweet wine and sugar. While still hot, blend in the xantana and pour into a siphon. Add 2 cream chargers and leave in the refrigerator to cool down. Before serving, shake the siphon thoroughly and extract slowly to create a perfectly smooth foam.

desserts

floating island with toffee sauce, vanilla anglaise and eggnog ice cream

eggnog ice cream

 45 min    serves 15

30 g milk powder
1 litre milk
480 g egg yolk
120 g sugar
80 ml cognac

1 Heat the milk powder in the milk until 85°C. Whisk egg yolk and sugar until white and creamy. Pour over the milk, whisking all the time or the egg mixture will start to cook. Pour the mix back into the pot and cook until it thickens at 75°–80°C. Strain and leave to cool.

2 Add the cognac when the mix is strained and cold. Churn in ice cream machine.

floating island

 15 min    serves 6-8

150 g egg white
60 g sugar
30 g butterscotch schnapps

1 Whisk egg white to soft peaks on medium speed, then slowly add sugar. Continue whisking until pearly white, then add the schnapps. Spray ceramic ramekins such as soufflé moulds or Chinese teacups with baking spray and fill with mix. Cook these one by one in a microwave at 50 percent power for 20 seconds. Leave to cool in the moulds, then unmould and cut into desired shape or leave whole. Serve a floating island with warm toffee sauce, cold vanilla Anglaise and a scoop of eggnog ice cream.

2 This recipe can be modified to suit your taste. For example, substitute the butterscotch schnapps with Malibu and then roll the floating island in coconut. Or substitute the Malibu with Grand Marnier or Cointreau and sprinkle with orange zest. The possibilities are endless once you have learnt the technique.

toffee sauce

30 min   makes 400 ml

200 g sugar
50 g cream
150 g butter
1 vanilla bean, split
   and scraped

1 Heat the sugar in a dry pan until a cognac-coloured caramel is formed. Add the cream, butter and scraped vanilla bean. Boil the mix for a few minutes to melt all the caramel again. Use a handheld blender and mix to a smooth and silky toffee sauce.

2 Can be served warm or cold.

vanilla anglaise

20 min   makes 250 ml

60 g cream
190 ml milk
1 vanilla bean, split
   and scraped
60 g egg yolk
60 g sugar

1 Bring cream, milk and scraped vanilla bean to boil. Keep aside. Whisk egg yolk and sugar until well combined but not white and fluffy. Pour the hot milk over the egg mix and whisk to avoid cooking the eggs. Pour the mix back into the pot and place over medium heat. Stir with a spatula until the mix thickens.

2 Strain the mix into a bowl and place over crushed ice to stop cooking.

champagne ice cream  45 min +1 hr serves 15

500 ml milk
250 g cream
250 ml champagne
240 g egg yolk
200 g sugar

1 Bring milk, cream and champagne to boil. Whisk egg yolk and sugar until white and creamy. Pour over the champagne milk. Whisk all the time or you will start to cook the egg mixture. Pour the mix back into the pot and cook until it thickens at 75-80°C.

2 Strain the mix and cool the mixture. Churn in ice cream machine.

caramelised milk ice cream 7+1 hr  serves 10

1 can condensed milk, 400 ml
1 litre ice cream base,
    10% sugar only

1 Place the can of condensed milk in a large pot filled with water, bring to boil and simmer the can in the water for 7 hours. You might need to top up with more boiling water during the cooking process. Allow the can to cool down overnight and use the following day. Mix the ice cream base with the condensed milk and churn in an ice cream machine.

ginger ice cream

45 min + 12 hr   serves 15

750 ml milk
250 g cream
150 g fresh ginger
    sliced on mandolin
100 ml ginger juice
240 g egg yolk
200 g sugar

1 Heat milk, cream, sliced ginger and ginger juice to 85°C. Whisk egg yolk and sugar until white and creamy. Pour into the ginger milk and cook until it thickens at 75°–80°C. Strain the mix and leave to mature in the refrigerator overnight. Churn in ice cream machine.

egg-free ice cream

1 hr   serves 15

1 litre milk
200 g sugar
170 g cream
40 g milk powder
50 g invert sugar /
    trimoline
1 vanilla bean
4 g ice cream
    stabiliser
2 gelatine leaves

1 Heat all ingredients to 85°C and keep mix at this temperature for 10 minutes to ensure mix is pasteurised.

2 Churn in ice cream machine.

Tip:
Add 25 g crushed coffee beans when you heat the mix in the beginning for café latte ice cream.

15 min   serves 20

gin and mint snow

1 litre water
50 g sugar
50 g bombay sapphire gin
2 tsp mint essence

1 Blend all together and freeze in a *pacojet container. Churn once when frozen. Use a fork to take out the "snow".

*Pacojets are not commonly used at home, but are essential in restaurants all over the world. They are fantastic machines and can be used for churning wonderful ice creams and sorbets.

bay leaf ice cream

1 hr   serves 15

1 litre milk
200 g sugar
170 g cream
40 g milk powder
50 g invert sugar / trimoline
15 g fresh bay leaves
4 g ice cream stabiliser
2 gelatine leaves

1 Heat all ingredients to 85°C and keep mix at this temperature for 10 minutes. This is to ensure the mix is pasteurised. Strain the mixture and cool over a bowl of ice. Churn in ice cream machine till smooth and frozen.

clafoutis and pastry cream

1 hr   serves 12

pastry cream

1 vanilla bean
500 ml milk
25 g flour
20 g wheat starch
160 g egg yolk
75 g sugar

1 Scrape vanilla bean into the milk. Whisk the flour and starch into the milk.

2 Cook over medium heat until thickened. Whisk yolk and sugar until combined, add the hot milk and return to the pot to cook until the mix has thickened. Pour into a container and place cling film on top to prevent a skin from forming. Cool on ice in the refrigerator.

clafoutis batter

500 g almond paste 50/50
   (50 percent sugar,
   50 percent almonds)
125 g butter
50 g flour
25 g milk powder
2 whole eggs
1 g salt

1 Place almond paste and pastry cream in a mixing bowl and mix with the paddle attachment. Add half the butter, flour and milk powder. Lastly, add eggs, then the rest of the ingredients. Mix until smooth, then strain through a fine mesh strainer.

2 This batter keeps for up to 5 days in the refrigerator. To bake clafoutis, spray 6-cm ramekins or aluminium cups with baking spray and fill with the batter. Bake at 190°C for 7–9 minutes. Once cooked, turn ramekin upside-down and gently ease the clafoutis out. Serve with pastry cream.

desserts

sorbet syrup

960 g sugar
110 g liquid glucose
10 g sorbet stabiliser
2 litres water

30 min
makes 3 litres

1 Place all the ingredients in a large pot and bring to boil. Leave to cool and keep until needed.

blackberry and grappa sorbet

1 kg blackberry purée
500 g sorbet syrup
50 ml grappa

30 min
serves 15

1 Blend all ingredients and strain, then churn in an ice cream machine.

physalis sorbet

45 min
serves 15

750 g physalis / gooseberries
750 g sorbet syrup
100 g banana purée

1 Blend all to a very smooth purée, then strain and churn in an ice cream machine.

guanaja chocolate sorbet

30 min   serves 15

500 g valrhona guanaja
   chocolate
1 litre aqua panna water
300 g sugar
2 gelatine leaves

1 Melt chocolate in a tall container. Warm the water and sugar to 60°C in order to melt the sugar. Soak the gelatine in ice water till soft, then add to the warm syrup. Blend all ingredients with a handheld blender. Strain, then churn in an ice cream machine.

desserts

strawberry or raspberry sorbet

 30 min  serves 15

650 g strawberry purée
 or 650 g raspberry purée
500 g sorbet syrup

1 Blend all ingredients and strain, then churn in an ice cream machine.

green apple sorbet

45 min   serves 10

600 g green apple purée
250 g green kiwi purée
425 g sorbet syrup

1 Blend all ingredients and strain, then churn in an ice cream machine.

blackcurrant and vodka sorbet

30 min   serves 15

1 kg blackcurrant purée
500 g sorbet syrup
50 ml vodka

1 Blend all ingredients and strain, then churn in an ice cream machine.

pear and vodka sorbet

1 kg pear purée
500 g sorbet syrup
50 ml vodka, with pear
   flavour if possible

20 min   serves 15

1 Blend all ingredients and strain, then churn in an ice cream machine.

fresh berries with breton sable biscuit, bourbon vanilla custard, wild strawberry and basil sorbet

breton sable 2 hr  serves 6

240 g unsalted butter
240 g castor sugar
120 g egg yolks
340 g flour
8 g sea salt
22 g baking powder

1 Using a mixer, whisk butter and sugar until white and creamy. Add egg yolk, then the dry ingredients. Chill the dough and roll to 5-mm thick. Bake at 160°C for 10 minutes, then cut into 4-cm circles and keep in airtight containers.

bourbon vanilla bean custard 2 hr  serves 6

500 g milk
1 vanilla bean, split and scraped
3 egg yolks
80 g sugar
40 g wheat starch
200 g whipped cream

1 Bring milk and vanilla to boil, then cool in the refrigerator. Whisk yolk and sugar till creamy. Whisk the starch into the milk and heat up. Cook for a few minutes to eliminate raw starch flavour. Add the milk to the yolk, then transfer to a pot to cook the yolk and thicken the custard.

2 Let the mix cool in the refrigerator, covered with cling film. When cold, fold in the whipped cream.

wild strawberry and basil sorbet

 30 min  serves 15

850 g wild strawberry purée
500 g raspberry purée
500 g sorbet syrup
22 g basil, leaves only

1 Blend all ingredients in a kitchen blender. Strain the mixture, then churn in an ice cream machine.

To serve:

Arrange fresh berries, Breton sable and vanilla custard as shown in image above, and top with a nice quenelle of wild strawberry and basil sorbet.

The first restaurant I worked in was Little River Winery & Restaurant in the Swan Valley, not far from Perth in Western Australia. The chef was my father and for over four years, I believe we had the best ice creams in Perth. But we did not have an ice cream machine! We made parfaits, and in lots of different flavours. I still make

passion fruit parfait
30 min   serves 12

400 g whipping cream
6 egg yolks
100 g sugar
100 g fresh passion
    fruit pulp
6 egg whites

1 Whip the cream to soft peaks.

2 Whisk the egg yolk with 50 g sugar until white. Add the passion fruit pulp to the egg mix. Whisk the egg whites with the remaining 50 g sugar until stiff peaks form.

3 Fold the cream into the egg yolk mix, and fold in the egg whites last.

4 Pour in a mould and freeze overnight.

5 This parfait is lighter than a usual parfait and is better eaten within a few days of making it; it can form ice crystals if stored for a longer period of time.

parfaits today, and love them just as much as when I first learned how to make them.

The method is simple and you don't need any expensive ice cream machines or Pacojets to achieve perfectly smooth frozen desserts at home.

prune and armagnac parfait

30 min · serves 8

300 g cream

30 g sugar

5 egg yolks

50 ml armagnac or cognac

100 g prunes, seeds removed
and soaked in hot tea with
a splash of cognac

1 Whip the cream to soft peaks and keep cold in the refrigerator.

2 Whisk the sugar and egg yolks until pale and creamy.

3 Add the Cognac and prunes to the egg yolk mix.

4 Fold the cream into the egg yolk.

5 Mix and pour into container or mould of choice and freeze for a minimum of 12 hours.

jivara parfait

30 min · serves 12

300 g valrhona jivara chocolate

8 egg yolks

50 g sugar

600 g cream, whipped

1 Melt the chocolate and cool to room temperature. Whisk the egg yolk and sugar until white and fluffy. Fold the melted chocolate into the egg mixture, then fold the cream into the egg/chocolate mix. Pour into a mould and freeze overnight.

terrine of custard baked bread, apples and raisins

20 min + 45 min baking time

serves 10

12 slices white toast bread

150 g melted butter

5 granny smith apples, peeled and sliced

2 tsp cinnamon powder

50 g sugar

100 g raisins, soaked in hot water for 1 hour

4 whole eggs

400 ml milk

1 Tbsp vanilla essence

1 Line a terrine mould with silicon paper.

2 Dip the bread in melted butter and place 3 slices at the bottom of the mould. Arrange a third of the sliced apples on top.

3 Sprinkle with cinnamon, then some sugar and raisins.

4 Mix the eggs with milk and vanilla essence; pour a third of the mixture over the apples so it just covers.

5 Repeat the steps 3 times so that you have a final layer of bread on the top. You should have a total of 4 layers of bread and 3 layers of apples.

6 Bake at 160°C for 45 minutes in a water bath.

7 Once cooked, remove from the oven and place under terrine press or weights to make sure the terrine holds when cut.

8 Allow to cool down in the mould. Then slice and toast under a hot grill before serving.

cinnamon and milk jellies

4 hr   serves 12

cinnamon jelly

3 gelatine leaves
200 g sugar
100 ml water
1 Tbsp cinnamon powder

1 Soak gelatine in ice water and bring the rest of the ingredients to boil. Add the gelatine and stir to melt into the mixture.

2 Pour mixture into 2-cm high pyramid-shaped silicone moulds, half-filling them. Cool to set before adding milk jelly mixture on top.

milk jelly

3 gelatine leaves
250 ml milk
50 g sugar
3 cinnamon sticks

1 Soak gelatine in ice water. Bring the rest of the ingredients to boil, then remove cinnamon sticks. Add the gelatine and stir to melt into the mixture.

2 Pour mixture on top of cinnamon jelly and fill the rest of the mould.

cinnamon espuma

30 min   serves 12

100 g cinnamon sticks
750 ml milk
350 g cream
200 g sugar
5 g xantana (*see glossary section under* texturas products)

1 Crush the cinnamon sticks in a mortar and pestle. Bring milk, cream, sugar and cinnamon to boil.

2 Blend in xantana, boil for 1 minute, then strain and pour into a siphon and charge with 1 gas cartridge. Chill the siphon and use when cold.

chocolates and *petits*

"Nothing is better than a few homemade treats to serve with a cup of coffee or tea when unexpected guests arrive..."

fours

egg-free tuile

30 min   serves 20

250 g liquid glucose
100 ml hot water
250 g butter
160 g sugar
250 g flour

1 Melt the glucose with the hot water, leave to cool to room temperature.

2 In a kitchen blender, add the butter and sugar first and blend until smooth. Add the flour to make a smooth paste, then slowly pour in the glucose and blend until smooth and soft. Keep in the refrigerator until set.

3 Spread the mix on a silpat mat and steam at 120°C for 3 minutes. Cut into desired shape and then bake at 190°C for 4–5 minutes until golden brown.

olive oil and wine biscuit

30 min   serves 50

250 ml red or white wine
500 ml extra virgin olive oil
150 g sugar
1 kg cake flour
2 tsp baking powder

1 Place wine, oil and sugar in a mixing bowl with a hook attachment. Sift flour and baking powder 3 times then add to mixing bowl. Do not over-mix the dough at this stage; just mix until it holds together.

2 Wrap the dough in cling film and rest in the refrigerator for 1 hour. Once the dough is rested, remove from the plastic and roll out to about 5-mm thickness. Using a round cutter, cut round biscuits and place on a greased baking tray and bake at 180°C for 6–7 minutes.

3 Remove the biscuits and cool on wire racks. Store in airtight jars, but they are best eaten the day they are baked. The dough keeps well for up to 4 days in the fridge.

notes *different oils, wines, sugars can be used in this recipe to change the flavour of the pastry.*

biscotti

2 hr · serves 50

- 100 g butter
- 160 g sugar
- 2 whole eggs
- 200 g roughly chopped roasted almonds
- 2 Tbsp crushed pink peppercorns
- 210 g flour
- 2 Tbsp baking powder

1 Whisk butter and sugar until creamy.

2 Add eggs one by one. Add in nuts and peppercorns, finally fold in flour and baking powder. Rest the dough for 30 minutes, then shape into 2 loaves on a silpat mat. Bake at 200°C for 11 minutes, then reduce heat to 175°C for 13 minutes.

3 Take out the biscotti loaves and rest for 15 minutes. Slice 5-mm thick and arrange on trays, and dry out at 100°C for 25 minutes.

chocolate lace tuile

10 hr prep + 5 min bake time · serves 20

- 75 g butter
- 190 g sugar
- 90 ml orange juice
- 4 Tbsp flour
- 15 g valrhona cocoa powder

1 Cream the butter and sugar with the paddle in a kitchen mixer. Add the orange juice, then sieved flour and cocoa powder. Whisk to combine and let rest overnight,

2 Spread thinly on a silpat mat and bake at 190°C for 4–5 minutes.

financier sponge cake

30 min · serves 50

- 200 g cake flour
- 1½ tsp baking powder
- 50 g valrhona cocoa powder *(optional)
- 500 g icing sugar
- 1 g sea salt
- 200 g almonds, roasted and ground with their skin on
- 500 g egg white
- 300 g nut butter

1 Sift the flour, baking powder and, if preferred, cocoa powder. Place the flour mixture, icing sugar, salt and ground almonds in a mixer fitted with the paddle attachment. Start adding the egg white, then the nut butter and mix until smooth. Keep in the refrigerator overnight before using.

2 Bake at 200°C for 9 minutes until golden and puffed.

notes

if using cocoa powder, sift it with the flour in the first step of the recipe.

macarons, french meringue method

1 hr

makes 40 macarons

125 g ground almonds
225 g icing sugar
105 g egg white
6 g egg white powder
25 g sugar

1 Heat your oven to 160°C. Sift together the ground almonds with icing sugar. Place the egg white, egg white powder and sugar in a kitchenAid and whisk on medium speed until it forms stiff peaks. This will take 5-6 minutes. Now, the crucial stage of this method starts. Fold in the almond and sugar mixture in 3 stages. Then keep pressing the batter to the sides of the bowl. This will give the batter lustre and make it glossy. Make sure you lift the batter from the bottom of the bowl to ensure it is well mixed. This should take about 15 fold-and-press motions. The batter is ready to pipe when it is thick and runs off a spatula slowly but evenly. Using a piping bag with a plain nozzle about 8-mm in diameter, pipe 3.5-cm rounds onto a silicon mat-lined baking tray. Once piped, let the rounds sit for 30 minutes to develop a crust.

2 Bake the macarons for 11–12 minutes. Remove from oven and let cool. Once cool, remove from baking sheet. Then fill with orange and vanilla curd (*see page 145*) or a chocolate ganache (*see page 139*).

macarons, italian meringue method

1 hr   makes 40 macarons

150 g ground almonds
150 g icing sugar
150 g sugar
40 ml water
55 g egg whites

1 Heat your oven to 180°C. Sift together the powdered almonds and icing sugar. Boil the sugar and water to 115°C, measured on a sugar thermometer. Place the egg white in a kitchenAid and whisk until soft peaks form. Once the sugar syrup is 118°C, pour the syrup into the bowl while still whisking. Continue to whisk until the temperature is just higher than body temperature. Remove the bowl from the mixer and fold in the almond and sugar mixture. Use a piping bag with a plain nozzle, about 8-mm in diameter and pipe 3.5-cm rounds onto a silpat mat-lined baking tray. Once piped, let the rounds sit for 30 minutes to develop a crust.

2 Bake the macarons for 11–12 minutes. Remove from oven and let cool. Once cool, remove from baking sheet. Then fill with orange and vanilla curd (see page 145) or a chocolate ganache.

3 For all types of macarons, it is best to use egg white that has been left in a bowl uncovered in the refrigerator for 5–7 days. This way, the egg white loses some of its moisture and will be more stable during whisking and baking.

star anise truffles

45 min   makes 35 truffles

100 g butter
450 g guanaja, valrhona 70 percent dark chocolate
400 g cream
80 g trimoline (inverted sugar)
10 g star anise

1 Melt butter and chocolate together. Bring cream, trimoline and crushed star anise to boil and strain over chocolate. Fill in dark chocolate shells.

orange grand marnier truffles

 45 min  makes 25 truffles

10 g cloves
125 g cream
80 g trimoline (inverted sugar)
1 orange, zested on microplane
6 g salted tangerine peel
150 g jivara, valrhona
   milk chocolate
50 ml grand marnier

1 Crush cloves and bring to boil with cream, trimoline, orange zest and salted tangerine peel. Melt Jivara, then strain cream into chocolate. Add Grand Marnier and fill in milk chocolate shells.

sichuan truffles

 45 min  makes 35 truffles

25 g sichuan peppercorns
40 g trimoline (inverted sugar)
50 g cocoa powder
180 g cream
40 g butter
250 g jivara, valrhona milk
   chocolate

1 Crush peppercorns and boil with all except the chocolate. Melt chocolate and strain the cream into chocolate. Fill in milk chocolate truffle shells.

vanilla and southern comfort truffles

45 min makes 25 truffles

2 vanilla beans, split and
   scraped
125 g cream
35 g unsalted échiré butter
80 g trimoline (inverted sugar)
75 ml southern comfort
150 g guanaja, valrhona
   70 percent dark chocolate

1 Bring scraped vanilla beans, cream, Échiré butter, trimoline and 50 ml Southern Comfort to boil. Simmer until it starts to thicken. Melt chocolate and pour in the cream. Stir to combine, then add remaining 25 ml Southern Comfort. Fill in dark chocolate shells.

whisky cardamom truffles

45 min — makes 35 truffles

10 g green cardamom pod
250 g cream
80 g trimoline (inverted sugar)
50 ml whisky
200 g guanaja, valrhona
70 percent dark chocolate

1 Crush cardamom and boil with cream and trimoline. Melt Guanaja, then strain the cream into chocolate. Add whisky, chill and fill in dark truffle shells.

cinnamon and lime truffles

45 min — makes 25 truffles

12 g cream

50 g cinnamon stick, very finely crushed

75 g trimoline (inverted sugar)

2 limes, zested on microplane

200 g ivoire, valrhona white chocolate

1 Bring cream, cinnamon stick, trimoline and lime zest to boil. Melt Ivoire and strain the cream into the chocolate. Fill in white chocolate shells.

POULIGNY SAINT PIERRE

Brenne Valley, France

Pyramid-shaped goat cheese made from alpine milk, rarefied sour and salty flavour. Once allowed to mature, natural mould will form. The cheese will be soft, moist and of fine texture.

BRIE DE MEAUX

Île-de-france, France

French cheese's king of kings.

Outstanding brie cheese that has been considered the finest cheese in Europe since the 19th century. Creamy, nutty, straw and white pepper flavour.

BRILLAT-SAVARIN

Normandy, France

Cow's milk aged 1-2 weeks. A triple cream brie, rich and faintly sour flavour. Named after French writer Jean Anthelme Brillat-Savarin. Pair with full-bodied reds for its creamy texture.

VACHERIN MONT D'OR

Massif du Mont d'Or

A winter cow's milk cheese, aged for a month and brine washed to build its flavour. Available only from September to March. Vacherin Mont d'Or is almost liquid when ripe and is eaten by scooping out the soft inner cheese. This is a very unique cheese with a rich creamy flavour.

ST AGUR

Monts du Velay, France

Cow's milk aged 60 days in deep cellars.

A blue double cream cheese, with a moist, rich and creamy texture. A subtle mild spicy taste. My absolute favourite blue cheese.

BEAUFORT

Haute-Savoie Mountains, France

Made from the milk of cows grazing exclusively on natural pastures off the mountain slopes. Flavour and scent of milk, butter and honey.

It takes 500 litres of milk to produce a 45kg cheese. This is one of the few cheeses that will pair well with white wine.

SURPRISE BAY CHEDDAR

Surprise Bay, King Island, Australia

Made from the milk of cows grazing on King Island outside Tasmania.

Aged for 12 months before being sold to allow time to develop its flavour. Crumbly texture with moist and mild sweetness.

RED SQUARE

Tasmania, Australia

Traditional washed rind cheese with a mild earthy aroma and lingering creamy taste.

As the cheese matures the interior turns custardy and the rind pungent and sticky.

DEEP BLUE

Tasmania, Australia

Indulgent blue cheese with a rich and robust character. Slightly crumbly and creamy texture that offers a gently sweet yet acidic taste. A well-balanced cheese from Tasmanian Heritage.

DOUBLE BRIE

Tasmania, Australia

This double brie is made with added cream which produces a mild and delicate nutty taste with a clean finish. It has a creamier and fuller flavour compared to traditional bries.

cheese *notes*

glossary

Trimoline is a sugar syrup obtained from sugar beets and cane sugar syrups. It is an uncrystallisable sugar that helps to preserve the shelf life of a product.

Isomalt is a natural sweetener, and an excellent sugar substitute. It can be used in a one-to-one ratio for normal sugar. It has the taste and texture of normal sugar but only half the calories. Isomalt is a low digestible carbohydrate made from beet sugar. It may be suitable for individuals needing to control their blood glucose and insulin levels, or for lower-calorie, healthier recipe alternatives.

Glucose is used in pastries, ice creams and pastry related recipes. It delays sugar crystallisation and keeps products and all pastry preparations from drying up for better product preservation. It gives sorbets a nice smooth texture.

Egg white powder is from egg whites that are pasteurised before being atomised into a fine powder. It helps to hold a better shape than fresh or frozen beaten white eggs. It also prevents granulation when mixed with fresh or frozen whites. Ideal to use when making macarons.

Wheat starch contains no gluten and works in a similar way to cornstarch, but I feel wheat starch has a cleaner flavour and sticks less to your mouth when you eat it. Here is the technical explanation: Wheat starch is made by commercial separation of pure wheat starch in a two-phase process. In the first phase, the wheat kernel is ground or converted into wheat flour by a dry milling process, like making normal plain flour. In the second phase, the ground wheat or the wheat flour is separated into its various components (starch, gluten, solubles, fibre) by a wet separation process.

Valrhona chocolates used in the recipes:

Araguani, 72 percent cocoa - A blend of Criollos and Trinitarios cocoa beans from Venezuela. A powerfully bitter base with strong liquorice, raisin and chestnut notes. Burnt aromas of honey and hot bread.

Guanaja, 70 percent cocoa. This is the best known of the Valrhona bitter dark chocolates. Valrhona has rediscovered the best cocoas, Criollos with the aroma of flowers and fruit, and the Trinitarios, typified by a strong bouquet to mix them all together. An exceptional dark bitter chocolate with floral notes and a powerful lingering intensity.

Jivara Lactee, 40 percent cocoa. A blend of Forasteros-type cocoa beans. Long-lasting flavour but not too sweet, its typical soft and chocolaty taste, with hints of caramel and vanilla, is derived from the blending of the best cocoa beans from South America, whole milk, cane sugar and a touch of malt. It's a delight for lovers of milk chocolate.

Ivoire, 35 percent cocoa. A slightly sugared white chocolate, well-balanced between milk and sugar, with delicate flavours and a very fine texture. All Valrhona products may contain traces of nuts, milk and egg proteins, gluten and peanut.

Texturas products used in the recipes:

Agar is extracted from a type of red algae (of the Gelidium and Gracilaria genera). Agar-agar is a gelling agent used in Japan since the 15th century. In 1859, it was introduced to Europe as a characteristically Chinese food, and at the start of the 20th century it began to be used in the food industry. It is a source of fibre and can form gels in very small proportions. It can be used to make hot gelatines. It comes as a refined powder.

Algin is a natural product extracted from brown algae (of Laminaria, Fucus, and Macrocystis genera, among others) that grow in the cold water regions of Ireland, Scotland, North and South America, Australia, New Zealand, South Africa, etc. Depending on the part of the algae that has been refined, the texture and Calcic reactivity of each alginate varies. For this reason, we have selected Algin as the ideal product for achieving spherification with guaranteed results. It comes as a refined powder.

Calcic is a calcium salt traditionally used in the food industry, for example in cheese making. Calcic is essential in the reaction with Algin that produces spherification. It is the ideal reactant for its high water solubility, considerable calcium content and, consequently, great capacity for producing spherification. It comes in the shape of small granules.

Lecite is a natural soy lecithin-based emulsifier, ideal for making airs and foams. This product, discovered at the end of the 19th century, was first produced for the food industry in the last century. It is useful in the prevention of arteriosclerosis and contains vitamins, minerals and antioxidants. Lecite is made from non-transgenic soy. It comes as a refined powder.

Metil is a gelifier extracted from the cellulose of vegetables. Unlike other gelifiers, Metil (with a metilcellulose base) gelifies when heat is applied. When cold it acts as a thickener. There is a wide range of viscosity in metilcelluloses, which affects the final result of the gelification. Metil has been chosen for its great gelifying power and reliability. It comes in powder form.

Xantana is obtained from the fermentation of corn starch with a bacteria (Xanthomonas campestris) found in cabbage. The result is a gum with great thickening power. It also has notable potential as a suspensoid, which means that it can maintain elements in suspension in a liquid without their sinking into it. It can also retain gas. It comes as a refined powder.

Pacojet is a machine that has revolutionised the blending and puréeing process for chefs. The machine mixes and purées deep frozen food directly in its frozen state, without thawing it, to produce a frozen and intensely natural-tasting mousse of extremely fine consistency. It is not a common machine for home cooks but I don't think I could ever work without a Pacojet again. It leaves your ice creams and sorbets perfectly smooth with no wastage from cleaning the machine. Maximum enjoyment with minimum work. But it comes at a price.